SO ALIVE AFTER 55

YOUR GUIDE TO THE FINER POINTS
OF ACTIVE ADULT LIVING

| SoAliveAfter55.com |

THERESA FOWLER WEBB

Created and published in collaboration with RoseDale Inc.
3030 Starkey Blvd, Suite 207
Trinity Florida 34655

ISBN: 978-0-9911200-9-3

Dedication

This book is dedicated to my Dad, who I wish was still here to share his love, his joy, and his strong yearning to always improve, learn, understand and discover.

He was the very proud father of four girls who surely drove him crazy as we were growing up. He sacrificed everything for his family and taught us the truest meaning of life... appreciation and gratitude.

In traditional Italian fashion, his box of treasure held unlimited and unconditional love for his family. Yes, indeed! My Dad certainly knew how to embrace life!

As Abraham Lincoln so eloquently stated, and my Dad wholeheartedly agreed-

> "And in the end,
> it's not the years in your life that count,
> it's the life in your years."

This was Dad's favorite quote and now I understand why.

THERESA FOWLER WEBB

Table of Contents

Preface

During my 20 years as Vice President and Project Manager of nine Active Adult Communities, I have accumulated knowledge through great experiences and heart-felt moments. I have helped and guided many Active Adults in understanding the Active Adult Lifestyle.

Many folks do not realize life does not have to be limited to a mere two or four weeks of vacation per year. It is a constant, active pursuit of LIFE. A realization of your dreams!!

With some sound knowledge and planning, you can enjoy the Active Adult Lifestyle, and that is why I have written this book – to provide insightful guidance to those interested in discovering and pursuing the opportunity of an Active Adult Lifestyle.

So here you are, this is retirement, so much time on your hands, nowhere to go, no one to hang out with… this can't be what you have looked forward to after all those years of working – whether in the work force or caring for your home and family. You and your partner are experiencing more "togetherness" than ever before.

Then without any warning whatsoever, thoughts pop up in your mind… *I wish the family was still growing… I should have stayed on and worked a few more years… I really miss lunches with my colleagues… I really wish I could take my family to the company picnic next week.* You find yourself faced with the frightful question... *What am I going to do tomorrow?*

When you were working or raising your family, you knew what to expect. Now, you have no idea. Without the structure of your previous day-to-day life, it may feel like you have nothing to live for.

These thoughts and feelings are not new to the "retiree" mindset.

The history of Active Adult Living goes back as early as the 1950's prompted by the same struggles you may be experiencing now.

Active Adult Living is Born

It all began in Youngstown, AZ, with Ben Schleifer, Francis Greer and Elmer Johns, who together developed 320 acres to build the first Adult Community. Ben Schleifer had the idea of a retirement community, Francis Greer had the land (a ranch), Elmer Johns brought the two ideas together, and *voila,* a concept was born. By 1955, they had 125 homes built, 85 lots sold and only 40 remaining. (1)

In 1960, Sun City, a planned community dedicated to Active Adult Living, was launched in Arizona. Del Webb Construction Company had established a great reputation in the construction industry with designs and the building of some of the fancy casinos in Las Vegas. It was one of the largest and fastest growing companies in the market.

Del E. Webb believed in the concept of affordable homes, resort style amenities, easy access to shopping, dining and entertainment, which offered a self-sustaining living environment. After much planning of his concept, he launched Sun City, a planned community dedicated to Active Adult Living on January 1, 1960, with the opening of models and the community to the public.

Great marketing strategies were implemented, including the media and press. The community captured the interest of folks from all over the country and brought over 41,000 people to the grand opening, and over 100,000 visitors over the weekend. 237 home were sold that weekend, and by the end of January 1960, 400 homes had been sold.

Del Webb not only launched a community on New Year's Day in 1960, he launched an innovative concept for Active Adult Living, which continues to flourish today.

"When I see what we've built, it is the most satisfying thing that's ever happened to me."   - Del Webb

He was extremely proud of what he brought to light in developing "active retirement living." (2)

Sun City West and Sun City Grand, by Del Webb Corporation, followed in the upcoming years – all retirement communities offering the Active Adult concept of living. A new way of living, with recreation, shopping, dining, service centers, and more, all at your fingertips.

Pulte Homes acquired Del Webb Corporation, and have retained the use of the Del Webb name for its retirement communities.

Active Adult Living Continues to Thrive

Today, many Builders across the country continue to

build communities around this very concept.

Some Builders offer smaller communities close to shopping, dining, and entertainment; while other Builders offer larger communities with shopping, dining, and entertainment within the boundary of the community.

Active Adult Communities offer many amenities, such as clubhouses where people gather to play cards, take 3-D art classes, or squeeze in a fitness class all while enjoying the care-free lifestyle of basically maintenance-free living.

Many *Active* Adult Communities are offered in warmer climates, more conducive to the recreational side of living. However, you can find an *Active* Adult Community even in the coldest of climates.

Active Adult Community living is truly unique. There are no "Musts" or "Must Nots." There are no "Dos" or "Do Nots." It is all about your "wants" and "desires." It's all about exactly what you enjoy, what you want to enjoy more, and who you want to enjoy it with.

Do you want a structured day full of activities like you had when you went out to work or worked in the home? Do you want to stimulate your curiosity? Are you ready to discover what you really enjoy and meet new friends?

You are the only one who can answer these questions. Only you can determine what you **MUST DO**, and what actions you need to take.

I want you to know all of this comes with the bonus of filling your heart, and best of all... staying in the game.

What do you want to do, to participate in, to enjoy, to experience, to feel, to become?

You picked up this book, and I hope that means you are considering the joys of Active Adult Living, but ultimately, the choice is yours.

Acknowledgements

It would take an entire book to express my appreciation, and I would probably still forget someone.

Thank you to all my customers, friends, and family – those who have always believed in and supported me. You have been the motivators of my drive and the source of my fortitude.

I am grateful for the "Two Maries" in my life –

My Mom who often reminds me I can accomplish anything at all once I put my mind to it. "Reach for the moon…and you will land among the stars," is an inspiring phrase I remember fondly from my childhood.

My mother-in-law who has accomplished much in her career and life. She is a source of inspiration to me, a woman of wisdom, and generously shares both.

My wonderful, incredible husband, Brad, consistently challenges me to be more than I ever imagine for myself! I adore him and admire his vision for our lives together. His support is relentless, and his love is limitless. I am truly blessed!

Jennifer, my amazing daughter, sees me as a bright light and appreciates my accomplishments. Chris, my son-in-law, keeps us entertained. He is the best Dad a Grandparent could ever hope for to my two wonderful grandsons. CJ and Jaxon, we are crazy about you! All of you make life more wonderful!

Katarina and Kassandra, my step-daughters, who are so incredible, it was difficult for me to ever be the "evil stepmom." Little Miss Ellie, our delightful granddaughter, you keep us on our toes with your charm.

My three sisters – my twin Angela, Linda, and Nancyanne – can overcome any obstacle in business or in life with their big hearts.

You have been an important part of my life – Ronnie, Tony, Annmarie, Christianne, Vincent, Paula, Mark, Bill, Morgan, Josh, Katie, Austin, Dean, Graeme, Debs, Sandy, Paul, Paulie, Michael, Rita, Stacy, Toni Michelle, Fran, Scot, Niki, Larry, and Barbara - I honor you in the spirit of family and human connection.

Many of my Valencia customers who have remained my friends over the past two decades, you know who you are; thank you for creating dynamic and energetic lives which inspired me to write this book.

Special thanks to the generous customers who volunteered your time and thoughts for the interviews in this book. Your wisdom will inspire and guide others seeking the ultimate in lifestyle.

I will remain forever grateful!

Introduction

I should have written this book years ago. It would have been such a great tool for many of my previous customers. I met with several of my 13,000 customers one-on-one over the course of 20 years to discuss a variety of the issues I have addressed in this book. There is no exact science to Active Adult Living. The content of this book serves as a "tour guide" to assist in navigating common stumbling blocks you might encounter as you transition to the retirement stage.

Imagine if there was no instruction manual on how to put together the bicycle you just purchased for your grandchild. You could probably figure it out, which might take some time, and the bicycle may ride smoothly. However, if you had an instruction manual with step by step instructions and an established sequence of tasks, the entire experience might be more pleasant, less time consuming, and less frustrating.

This book is your instruction manual, focused on the transformation to the Retirement stage of LIFE. As a retired VP of nine Active Adult Communities for two decades, I will act as your guide to discover the new lifestyle awaiting you.

Take the journey with me through this book of personal, candid interviews. Those who have found their way and are currently living the life they love share their experiences and anecdotal pearls of wisdom to help you avoid some of the "pitfalls" they've encountered. They now enjoy a life full of activity and emotional support, all because they simply chose to live in an Active Adult Community.

The *WHAT* is not nearly as important as discovering your *WHY*. At the start of our journey, I will help you understand how important it is to focus on your *WHY* **first**.

Many people at this stage of their life find their *WHY* to be *community* which makes sense when you consider where we come from. Back in the day when we were children, one of the most important things in our lives was our friends.

Then we grew up.... focused on our careers or raising families or both. Here we are at the retirement stage of our lives... and now friends are back in play. Friends to laugh with, friends to cry with and friends to simply chat with. A *sense of community* is one of the great benefits that comes with Active Adult Living.

Through the course of my career, I had the pleasure of meeting with many customers and have laughed and cried with them. They shared their concerns, their fears and their joys. As the years went by, I realized many had similar concerns.

One day there were customers requesting to meet with me. They didn't have an appointment, so I was not prepared and had no idea what we would be discussing. I led them into my office, we sat down and they both started talking.... with a lot of emotion and anxiety. I listened very carefully to understand the issue and started to formulate the resolution.

Their issue was somewhat common... they were

moving far away from their friends and family and had no idea *how* to begin their new lives. I excused myself from the meeting and walked into the display area of the office. I had recognized some customers in the office prior to our meeting who were already enjoying their new life and asked them to join us in my office.

They were happy to... I introduced them and that was just the beginning... they shared their new experiences, their joys and excitement and most importantly, what they felt to be rewarding about living in an Active Adult Community. You probably know the end of the story.... they are great friends now and on occasion would stop by to see me to chat.

I was fortunate enough to be a part of the wonderful "human connection" by pairing those who are currently living the Active Adult Lifestyle with those who are just starting out. This book captures the essence of that connection by sharing interviews of real-life people who are currently living the lifestyle. My hope is, you can calm any fears you may have by reading how they overcame theirs and understand – you are not alone.

I share this story because during my 20 years, I noticed many who were faced with moving to a new area, or different state, experienced anxiety. The unknown is enough to cause a bit of fear. We are human and yes, we feel emotion strongly. I have found this fear can be overcome, and has been overcome, when excitement comes into play.

Another common concern for those contemplating or making the decision to live in an Active Adult Community is the *Lifestyle*. Many are not aware of the opportunities presented when joining an Active Adult Community. The social events offered (depending on the individual community) *encourage* and *foster* friendships simply through participation.

"It's all about the Lifestyle," I quote throughout the book... but what does this mean? It means something different to everyone... because you and only you have the definition and meaning... yes you. It can mean anything you want... simply put, it's your choice to participate or not participate in as many activities, events or clubs as you want. Make loads of friends, become involved in the community... and on and on. The first step is often the hardest, but I am here to guide you on every page of this book. There is no need to experience the fears, frustrations, and overall confusion of not knowing what to do next. You are not alone in unchartered territory. It's all here in a step-by-step how-to guide and the journey begins with your *WHY* in Chapter one, "Is this for me?"

CHAPTER 1

IS THIS FOR ME?

ONE ~ Is This For Me?

A question asked by many, and one I have been asked personally–numerous times over the past 20+ years, *WHAT is an Active Adult Community and WHY would I want to live in one*?

What makes an Active Adult Community different and why does it appeal to so many people? Is an Active Adult Community for me? Will I like a community specifically designed for Adults?

The answers are not quite as simple as the questions, since the answers in part can only be found within *YOU!*

The different stages of life have brought us here... to the retirement stage.

When we are in our 20's we are just starting out in the world, building towards something, (not sure what) and constantly working toward the next step; maybe marriage and then possibly children.

In our 30's, many of us are very busy raising our wonderful children, working diligently on building our careers, and then before we know it, we are in our 40's. The kids are grown up, our careers have taken off, and we have found what we feel is our place in this world. In many cases, the children we raised are going off to college, getting married and/or moving forward to begin their lives.

Maybe you took a less traditional path, not spending a million plus dollars per child. No matter which path you chose, suddenly you have entered your 50's and life is really changing. Spencer Johnson, M. D. famously said, "Who moved my cheese?" and I concur!

So here we are, and many of us are searching for *something*. We don't really know what that *something* is. Perhaps it is the life, the fun, and the joy which comes from living among like-minded people in the same stage of life as our own.

It is time to ask yourself, "Is an Active Adult Community for ME?" as well as a few key questions about the lifestyle you desire to live. Are you interested in exploring your inner most passions, forging new friendships, becoming engaged in a variety of activities, or possibly utilizing your leadership skills for community type services? Do you want to relax and just sit by the pool? What about simply taking in the beautiful sunset while sitting on your patio and sipping a glass of wine? Can you feel a sense of satisfaction? Can you taste the possibilities? This is your time, and you have not only earned it, you deserve it!

I have found during my 20 plus years of working with the Active Adult, that many folks at this stage of life share similar traits and interests, in addition to feeling kindred emotions. One very common reaction is to experience a bit of fear along with a fabulous feeling of excitement.

After all, moving, to a new neighborhood, to another state or possibly across the country, can be a bit emotional. Leaving established and long-standing relationships can be difficult and tax your heart. Familiarity of the area you are leaving may also play a role in your emotions. You are not alone with these feelings.

It might be comforting for you to know many like-minded people in the community you may be joining, have most likely been in the same frame of mind. They have experienced a knot in their stomach, but others who have taken the leap helped them navigate through this monumental life transition. In the end, the experience was pleasurable and lifetime friendships were formed. *This is where it all begins.*

A brief description of an "Active Adult Community" could be as simple as a "playground for adults", with people from all cultures and backgrounds enjoying the best life has to offer.

Maintenance free living is another huge benefit offered in many adult communities. With the lawn, hedges and trees maintained, all you have to do is sit back and relax. Those are examples of some of the *tangible* advantages of living in an Active Adult type Community.

The *tangible* advantages?? You may be wondering what I am talking about! Let's consider the multiple *intangibles!*

These are the benefits which are not visible, but readily available to you when living in a community which is designed to provide a desired Lifestyle. Forming new relationships is one of the most powerful *intangibles* when living in an Active Adult Community.

Opportunities to form relationships which can flourish through the years are abundant and at your fingertips, especially when there are numerous clubs to join, activities to participate in, lectures to attend and a variety of social events offered in your community of choice.

You might be asking yourself, *why is that so important*? Another difficult question but again, the answer lies *within you.* I have certainly run across those who did not think they wanted to be a part of an Active Adult Community, possibly because of the fear which lurked within them about leaving their other life behind.

Questions would creep up; will I fit in, will I make new friends, will the community welcome me?? Of course, in the end, their fears were unfounded. After moving into the community and experiencing some of the activities and social gatherings, they quickly realized they did not leave their other life behind at all, but rather added another facet to their lives. They had new friends and new interests; and enjoyed sharing all their new experiences and excitement with all their friends, both new and old. They were filling their lives with new friendships, creating new memories, and so much more.

Do you want to explore your passions? Do you have a desire to be more active, get involved, form a club, participate in a game of bridge or canasta? No, not for you? That's okay. How about a nice afternoon just lounging by the pool and having some lunch with friends?

If you feel a sense of anticipation when thinking about

the possibilities of what is available, you should consider Active Adult Community living. Still unsure if this is for you? Keep reading and in chapter 9, I have provided a prequalifying questionnaire to guide you in your decision.

Interview with Jack Stewart - resident of an Active Adult Community.

Why did you move to an Active Adult Community and what inspired you?

It's really a funny story. My wife went out shopping one day with her girlfriend and came home, only to tell me she put a deposit on a home in an adult community, along with her girlfriend. She went out shopping for a dress and came home with a house.

At the time, we had been living in our home for nine years, which was in a small community with a small clubhouse, no gated front entrance, and no social activities to enjoy. My wife really was interested in socializing and meeting new people, forging new friendships, and having camaraderie with neighbors. She wanted to play cards, have block parties, and get involved in community affairs. It was obvious to her an Active Adult Community would fill the void she was so needing to fill. I had no idea I would grow to love it as much as I do...no idea at all.

Once I settled in, it became clear to me some of the residents were part-time residents who were at their other homes a portion of the year. They needed someone to watch over their homes while they were spending time at their other homes. Many of these "snowbirds" needed someone to walk thru the home once a week, keep an eye on the exterior, the irrigation, the yard, etc., and report any issues to the appropriate parties. So, I started Home Watching and offered my services to those individuals interested. Before I knew it, I was no longer retired. Quite the contrary, I was very busy again. The business kept growing for 20 years until my recent retirement. I had over 100 clients when I retired.

When we purchased our home, we were one of the first residents to move into our community. There were no activities yet and no clubs formed, since there was not an abundance of residents yet. We chose to be the leaders of our block; we created and organized social events, block parties and meet-n-greet events. We knew these types of activities would bring people together and felt strongly that they were a MUST. Those activities helped form the culture of the community and brought people together which we feel avoids the forming of clicks….and nobody wants to deal with clicks.

Pearls of Wisdom shared by the interviewee

The most important piece of advice I would like to share is: YOU MUST HAVE A VOICE. Do not move into a community and hibernate. Take part in what is happening, what is going on around you, and in the community. You WILL STAY YOUNGER.

SOCIALIZE – if you don't socialize and you don't meet your neighbors, you will be stuck in a RUT! We absolutely love living in an Active Adult Community, and it has been over 20 years….and we still have lots to do and enjoy!

My Take

The message I received from this interviewee was one person in the relationship knew exactly what she wanted in a community, while the other person in the relationship wasn't searching and was satisfied with their current lifestyle. Even though he wasn't really looking for a change; he stumbled upon an enormous opportunity and built an entire business, while enjoying an active lifestyle. The business created even more opportunities to meet people and begin relationship building.

As a couple, they were instrumental in forming the various activities and social events which enabled the residents to connect and get to know each other. They were the pioneers in their community and helped develop the culture of the community through Human CONNECTION!

Interview with Tali Shaye – resident of an Active Adult Community.

Why did you move to an Active Adult Community?

I liked the floorplan of the home. I fell in love with the flow of one of the homes, it just captivated me. I wasn't familiar with Active Adult Communities or what they offered, or how it was different from other communities. I was moving 1,200 miles away from my friends and family and had lived in a beautiful home. What did I know about Active Adult Communities? I was only 53, but I felt I was ready to consider this lifestyle.

Being the curious person I am, I asked the salesperson what my expectations should be regarding the Active Adult Lifestyle. He took some time to explain the various activities which were offered: the clubs I could join if I wanted, the headliner shows I could attend, and the tennis. The idea of tennis was quite appealing to me.

I still wanted more information. My curious nature led me to asking random people I met at the model or sales center, the same question again and again. I didn't realize it at the time but by approaching those folks, I was cultivating future relationships.

It was NEW, so I would be NEW. I wanted a large community because you can make a large community small by getting involved, but you cannot make a small community large.

It's VERY IMPORTANT to make friends. It becomes second nature when you have so much in common with other residents: you are in the same age category and stage of life, you have common interests, and the most important commonality is they want to meet people and make new friends as well.

I did have a wave of fear, I certainly asked myself a few questions. Will I like the people in this community? Will I make friends? Will they like me? Will we have similar interests? I'm not sure the word FEAR really explains how I felt. I think the phrase "fear of the unknown" is more appropriate.

I was leaving my family, my two adult children, and I was leaving everything I knew; but I TOOK A LEAP OF FAITH and trusted my heart that this was the community for me.

I was right! In the beginning, the first residents of the

community would get together to meet, socialize, get to know each other and exchange phone numbers. It expanded even more when I realized many of the residents I had met at these events, also previously lived in the same area where I had lived. Some of them even had part-time homes remaining in the area, as I did.

We now have friends who live in both communities. What a great surprise.

A NEW BEGINNING would be the way I would reference my life in an Active Adult Community. I immediately got involved with tennis and I was getting pretty good. Before long, I was asked to Captain the Tennis League, which was a travelling team.

I also joined a couple of Philanthropic Clubs and feel so wonderful about what I was accomplishing by offering my help to those in need. I belong to a couple of groups who get together to play cards and I am having the time of my life. Just love it. Like I said, a new beginning.

Pearls of Wisdom shared by the interviewee

People are people. Keep in mind, when sharing information, private is private. Absolutely be social but what information you don't want shared, don't share it. Keep in mind that in the community, everybody knows everybody.

The most important thing I could share is to be FRIENDLY WITH EVERYONE. When new folks move into the community, introduce yourself, and welcome them to the community. Have fun with it; you will *certainly make lots of new friends.*

My Take

The opportunity of a new beginning, new friends, new activities and new ways to live one's life - WOW, that is so powerful! To ponder the thought of a new beginning and letting your imagination help build your new life can be quite invigorating and energizing.

The interviewee was certainly fueled by POSSIBILITY. The multitude of possibilities which could impact her life, change her story and live her life abundantly. She embraced her opportunity and carefully crafted her life, the way she wanted it to be. How awesome it that?

"You only live once,

but if you do it right, once is enough."

- Joe Lewis

CHAPTER 2

LOCATION, LOCATION, LOCATION

THERESA FOWLER WEBB

TWO ~ Location, Location, Location

We have all heard the saying; *Location, Location, Location*, but do we really understand the meaning behind such a statement? Is the statement purely referencing the neighborhood where your home is located, or could it be more about the city or even possibly the area of the country? Actually, it may be all of those things.

When you are researching the location, where you might be interested in living, take into consideration where you are coming from. Staying true to your heart will help you determine where your new life will be heading... in more than one sense.

Are you moving from a metropolitan area; or from across the country in a quiet little town, where everyone knows everyone? Those are two extreme examples but represent some of the choices you will be faced with when determining the location for your new life.

If you are from a quiet remote town, then you may want to avoid living near a noisy city. Or perhaps not! Maybe that is just what you are looking for; a vibrant area, full of life and entertainment options, with lots of people constantly around enjoying life.

If you live near the ski slopes and enjoy skiing as a *major* part of your life; a sunny and warm climate might not be a consideration for you. Perhaps you feel it may be time for a climate change and the beach seems very attractive to you for your new life. A walk along the ocean shore may not have been available to you previously, but now you can make it part of your new life.

As you consider all the options and alternatives available to you, selecting the perfect geographic area will serve as a strong foundation for your search. Once this is determined, you can start to research the area which would become your new neighborhood.

Next you may want to explore the area for proximity to entertainment, cultural arts centers, airports, seaports, places of worship, shopping, dining, and health care facilities. Also look at population, crime rates, and growth rate of the area, and any other information which might affect your decision about the area.

If you dine out frequently, a thorough appraisal of nearby restaurants and dining options may be in order. If shopping is something you enjoy, do you prefer browsing in the malls or boutique type shopping? Do art galleries and museums hold a special place in your heart? With some research regarding nearby malls, museums and quaint boutique shops, you will reap the benefit of knowing places of specific interest are nearby for your enjoyment.

Go a little deeper and closer to "home" by asking yourself this question: are you okay living near some noisier areas in the neighborhood such as the tennis courts or pickleball courts? Many folks are accustomed to noisy areas, especially those from metropolitan areas, but you may not be one of them. If not, you may want to avoid the noisier type areas of the community.

Other neighborhood or development questions might be: are you looking for a serene back yard view to enjoy while lounging on the patio, perhaps with a garden or lake view? Do you want a large yard, or would you prefer to be close to your neighbors? What about living in a gated community, are you interested in living in a community which offers a gatehouse? These are some important questions you may consider asking yourself which will assist you in narrowing your search.

Is your goal to live in proximity of family? This is a very common reason for relocating to a new area, and why not? Family binds people together and is a connection like no other that can be very strong. Or, you may long to be near old friends who are thoroughly enjoying their lives? Take some time to ask them questions and listen to what they have found exhilarating in their new lives. This factor can also play an important role in your decision.

Now, there are just three things for you to do... homework, homework, and homework. It sounds like a bunch of work, but don't fret, I have done a lot of the homework for you. You will find a questionnaire at the back of this book to assist with the process.

Moving to an Active Adult Community is a life changing decision, take the time to plan for the "rest of your life." Adventure awaits you! Are you ready?

My hope is by the end of this book, you will be more informed and much better equipped to understand the location, the type of home, the community style of choice, and the amenities and conveniences you value, and all before you take one physical step.

Interview with Ellen Adler – resident of an Active Adult Community.

Why did you buy in an Active Adult Community?

We went to visit my Aunt, who lived in an adult community. We were very impressed with the location, and equally as impressed with the overall community and how she lived her life in general. After returning home, we didn't think about it much, as we were on the younger side, still plugging away at our careers and working hard.

We returned to that community when my Aunt passed away in 2008. It was interesting, I felt the same feelings again; I was very impressed with the community and the Lifestyle the community had to offer. It felt so good.

This community offered a nicer lifestyle than where we were currently living in the Northeast. It was much prettier, much newer, and so fresh! It was more of a "gentle" lifestyle, no one was in a rush, like where we currently were living. What a great feeling. And let's not forget the warm weather. Although there are four seasons in the Northeast, it is such a short period of time to really enjoy each season. Not really a climate conducive to a lot of outdoor activities.

We took the plunge and purchased a home close to where my Aunt had lived. We were so excited, even though we were going to be "snowbirds" and continue living our primary lives in the Northeast until we were ready for retirement. Our dream was to be able to have both homes and spend at least three months a year at our second home enjoying our dream life.

That was almost ten years ago, and in the last few years, we have increased our time at our second home from three months per year to four months. We are looking to increase the time even more each year until we are ready for retirement.

We just love it. We feel the quality of life is better at our second home and we have no desire to leave. We travel back and forth a lot, even though I don't travel well, but it is so worth it, and I wouldn't trade it for the world.

We have the best of both worlds! Someone recently said to me, and I quote "any day you wake with a Palm Tree, is a Good Day", and I wholeheartedly agree. I think about that simple statement and realize how very lucky I truly am.

Pearls of Wisdom shared by the interviewee

Follow your heart, that is what we did, and we wouldn't do anything different. Not a thing! We were on the younger side when we purchased in the adult community, and people looked at us like we were crazy. We bought in an Active Adult Community to LIVE.

We have made phenomenal friends and we love the lifestyle so much that we sold our primary home and purchased in an adult community in the Northeast as well. We wanted to experience the same type of feeling. We were so involved and engrossed in the community at our secondary home, that we are *determined to feel the same way about our primary home.*

We love our life, what's not to love? It's really a state of mind. We hang out at the café and just chat with our friends for hours. I live to be happy and looking outside at the beautiful sunshine, listening to the birds chirping, is a good part of the tremendous happiness, I call LIFE.

My Take

Taking the plunge when they made the decision to purchase in an Active Adult Community, greatly impacted their lives. They were not retired, or even near that stage of life, but they have found what many retired people may be seeking...the ultimate in life and in lifestyle.

Making friends and keeping busy with lifestyle activities is the secret to their happiness. So much so, they were determined to duplicate what they had found emotionally in their vacation home. Once they arrived at this community, they knew where they wanted to live and enjoy life. They felt that "feeling" from the moment they entered thru the gate.

Interview with Patrick Johnson – resident of an Active Adult Community.

Why did you buy in an Active Adult Community?

It's a funny story. I am a veteran, and the day I returned from Vietnam, it was freezing cold in the Northeast. That was the day I set my sights on relocating our lives in a warmer climate. And we did. We took the leap and moved the family to a warmer climate for a portion of the year.

We originally purchased a home in a County Club type community of all ages. We lived there for 10 years, and before we knew it, our kids were all grown up. Our daughter's impending wedding prompted us to look for a larger home, in order to accommodate all the company which we anticipated.

We did not focus on the Active Adult Community because we had not heard of the concept. We were getting ready to buy elsewhere before we made our final decision to purchase in an Active Adult Community.

While we were living in the family community, we would occasionally drive to a particular area for shopping, dining and other activities; which made us think more about possibly living in the area. It certainly offered the things that were important and attractive to us.

One day we decided to take a drive and stopped in a new home community sales office to see what an Active Adult Community was all about.

Well, it didn't take us long, we instantly fell in love. We were made to feel very welcome by the staff, but what really made the difference in our buying decision was when we met other people in our age group while we were browsing through the models. They were looking for basically the same things we were.

We didn't know anything about the Lifestyle, but it sure sounded tempting. It was all new to us. There was so much to do - activities, clubs, shows, the list went on and on. The tropical feeling of the overall community was a major factor when making our decision.

It was such an exciting time for us. We purchased a Brand New home, selected the colors of cabinets, floors, etc. and we watched our home being built every day. It was a great and inspiring experience. During the six-month building process, we met more people who purchased homes in the community and we got to know them also. It was like a Rebirth.

To this day, eighteen years later, the community is very well kept, and best of all, we have great neighbors. It's like one GIANT PARTY. We go to the pool at night and meet people and just hang out and talk. We just love that. It's just so easy.

Pearls of Wisdom shared by the interviewee

We love this portion of our lives. What keeps us here is our great neighbors, the people in general, and the maintenance free type living.

Some folks need to chill out, and they would be happier. We have made so many new friends, and we simply enjoy our life.

My Take

He wanted to take his family to live, at least a portion of the year, in a warmer climate, which he accomplished immediately. Eventually they became full time residents in a community concept they didn't even know existed. The Active Adult Lifestyle was very new to them, but they knew they were attracted to the area, which meant a great deal to them.

They thoroughly enjoyed watching their home being

built and engaging in the adventure daily. Another very exciting time for them.

They have thrived in their community by making lots of friends and simply enjoying life for over 18 years. Like the interviewee said, "It's Like One GIANT Party."

"Where you are coming from is
as important as where you are going."
- Theresa Fowler Webb

THERESA FOWLER WEBB

CHAPTER 3

BRAND NEW

THERESA FOWLER WEBB

THREE ~ Brand New

Congratulations, you have now reached the "narrowing your search" portion of your journey. You should feel exhilarated that you are ready to move on to the next step of *outlining* your new and exciting lifestyle. Here you will pinpoint the major factors which will be significant when creating your strategy and for moving forward.

First, let's talk about the area or region. After considering and analyzing all the options available to you, the time has come to narrow down those locations. Which ones offer the most personal value to *you*?

Did you decide you want to live in an area that has been growing and thriving? How close do you want to be to your family? Within a few miles, or within a few hour's drive? Does the area offer you proximity to places of interest to you? Can you picture yourself living and building a life in the area? If you answered yes to any of those questions, you are ready for the next step.

What is the next step? To most folks, it would be to search for the community which offers the personal interests and value that would optimize their lifestyle of choice. Whether it be a very active lifestyle in a community full of activities and clubs or simply a community that offers just tennis or golf. Sounds easy, right? It certainly can be very easy and even rewarding if you narrow your search and prioritize by *your* level of interest and *your* level of value.

Okay, now you are ready to concentrate on the next subject: **Community.** Is a Brand New community or a well-established community most appealing to you?

Are you the pioneering type who embraces the new and unknown and finds it exciting, or do you prefer a more established and predictable environment? Let's break it down and consider the benefits of what each has to offer.

New Community – in most cases, a new community would refer to *everything* being newly developed. Depending on your Builder or community, the home can be customized to your individual taste.

Are you interested in forming and establishing clubs and activities to kick off the lifestyle in the community? Does the idea of collaborating with other residents, to create and implement a newsletter, appeal to your sense of adventure and creativity? These are just a few of the basic "start-up" tasks you can participate in should you purchase in a new community.

If new construction appeals to and you are dedicated to building new, then you need to research the Builder who will be constructing your new home. Learn about the Builder's reputation for customer care. You want to know that the Builder you choose will "be there" to take care of any issues after you move into your new home, as well as in the future. Read reviews and blogs to help you get a good feel for their company culture, and public opinion of the Builder. This will help you determine if the Builder will meet your expectations.

Of course, the financial stability of the Builder is important. Is the Builder well capitalized or in debt? This should play a key role in your decision. Equally important is how long the Builder has been in the business of home and community building. Gain a better understanding of the Builder, the communities they have built, how many have they built, and where the Builder is headed. This will ultimately act as your guide during your search and possibly prevent disappointments in the future.

A great place to start your research on the Builder you are considering is to take a drive through other communities they have built. Pay careful attention to the entrances, beautiful landscaping, and decorative elements which add dimension to the community. Look at the elevations of the homes and how they relate to the overall scheme and warmth of the community. Notice if it is all in harmony.

Remember, when purchasing a newly constructed home, there may be many other homes in various stages of construction surrounding you for some time. While not permanent, there may be some temporary inconveniences.

This may include some debris on the roadways, some common areas which are not completed or landscaped, street lighting that is not installed, the gatehouse may not be built or operational, or the clubhouse may not be finished.

Because no one has mastered the art of *quiet* home building, the potential of some noisy activities may be ongoing for a while. This may include, loud generators, trucks dropping off building materials, hammering, and various construction noises.

An afternoon drive to one of your Builder's completed communities is an item for your **MUST DO** list. It is imperative to visually see the end results of a finished community, unless your home is one of the last built in your chosen community. This exercise contributes to the overall feel of "community" you will sense. Your goal is to gain a solid sense of the quality of the finished product and neighborhood.

I *strongly* suggest speaking with residents in the community. Ask them how they feel the Builder rated on a scale from one to ten, during their building experience. Have some questions ready and ask if they were treated fairly and with honesty during the building process. Ask how happy they were with the Builder at the end of their home building journey.

Speaking with individuals who have already been through the experience, will be one of your most informative and valuable forms of research. You will be surprised how much people will share with you, whether it was a good experience or a bad one.

Be sure to also stop at the clubhouse if there is one, so you can see first-hand what's going on. Note how many people are participating and enjoying a craft or activity and how many are taking a dip or just lounging by the pool. Pick up some flyers or ask for a newsletter.

Take a moment to ask some of those folks about the lifestyle offered in the community, the entertainment, clubs, parties, and shows. Ask how involved they are and what they would change, if anything, should an opportunity present itself. This effort on your part comes with no cost to you but will be a priceless addition to your decision-making process.

If you are planning on selling your current home, building a new home can serve as a good timing mechanism for you. When you are building your new home from the ground up (no pun intended) it will take some time to complete. This will give you some time to sell your current residence.

Keep in mind however, should you sell your current home faster than expected, the chances of "speeding up" the construction of your new home may not be a possibility. Should this occur, you will need to make the necessary adjustments to your living arrangements on your own. In most cases, there is no obligation of the Builder to assist unless this subject is addressed and is clearly defined as the Builder's obligation in the Purchase Contract which you signed at the time of your purchase.

Of course, the ultimate timing would be to plan the closing of your current home and the closing of your new home simultaneously. Sounds like an easy task but it may be a bit more complicated than meets the eye.

And while we are on the subject, a *careful review* of the Builder's Purchase Contract should be on your **MUST DO** list. You should be familiar with your responsibilities, the deposit requirements, timeframes of such, and all the terms and provisions as well as the responsibilities of the Builder. Everything you need to know is in the Purchase Contract, so it makes sense to have your attorney review it with you.

You should now feel like you have a better grasp of the details of purchasing a newly constructed home in a community.

New home construction is a dance of excitement versus some inconveniences. However, excitement will be the last one remaining on the dancefloor when the new community is completed.

Interview with Norm Lichtenstein – resident of an Active Adult Community.

Why did you move to an Active Adult Community?

The price-range, the age restriction, and very importantly, the reputation of the Builder. We purchased a newly constructed house.

We saw many homes, in many different areas, but we seemed to gravitate toward this particular community. The community just felt right for us. I remember driving down the road, and turning the car around while telling my wife, "We are going back to that community and placing a deposit on the home we love." We were anxious to leave the inclement weather where we currently lived, in addition to escaping the high taxes of the area. We wanted something more. We wanted a lifestyle and we were in love with the idea of being able to participate as much as we wanted or as little as we wanted, in a community which offered all types of activities.

The social aspect was extremely attractive to us. Everyone in the community is in your age group, so you could have a thousand friends, or not.

We did have some worries about selling our existing home, considering the market at the time. We were patient and it took a while, but it all worked out well. We were so full of excitement and ready to make the move.

Even though I was comfortable and familiar with the current area where I lived, we felt we needed a break. So, we took the leap and did it... we made the move.

We didn't know who we were going to meet but we found in an Active Adult Community, you just meet people. We are not friends with everyone in the community, but we have made a lot of friends. I find that everyone we meet has a unique story, as we have. But the commonality of so many aspects of our lives are so apparent. For instance, some were feeling guilt and anxiety over the thought of leaving their grandchildren. But as I had previously shared with family members and now others, this was OUR TIME!

The Lifestyle is the key, and it was our main reason for becoming part of an adult community. We both love to socialize, so a community offering an array of activities and social gatherings, along with a resort style setting, was the major factor in our decision to purchase the home in the Active Adult Community.

Pearls of Wisdom shared by the interviewee

If you are purchasing a home which will be newly constructed, take the time and plan for the future. Some folks decide to wait on added features, thinking they could just add them later instead of having the Builder include them, not realizing what a huge undertaking it would be. My advice to those building a newly constructed home is to do everything you want to do, add in those options, do it while the home is being constructed by the Builder. It's so much easier... and definitely a bit more - timely.

ASK QUESTIONS. Be sure you are asking people who are reliable on the subject matter. Do some research. When considering the size of your home, think about the future. Will your kids come to visit? Will they all come at once? This will help you determine how many bedrooms you will really need.

My final statement... It's like going to Camp. Adult Camp.

My Take

Building a Brand New home can be quite an exciting venture. The process of selecting the cabinets and the countertops, the flooring and the fixtures, to suit your taste and liking, can be very rewarding. You may find the process simple and fun, while others may find it a bit challenging. A Designer/Decorator may be a consideration if you require a little assistance with the coordination of the colors and materials to be chosen for your home.

Another great thing about a newly constructed home is you may have several floor plan options to choose from. There might be possible structural options, such as adding an extra bedroom, extending the garage, or adding a swimming pool, just to name a few. These are the sort of options the interviewee was referring to when he recommended adding them into the home WHILE the home is being constructed.

If you are on the fence about a certain option, and the option is structural in nature, I highly recommend you add the option through the Builder, while the home is being constructed. This will be a far less invasive process and you will get the options you desire. I cannot tell you how many horror stories I have heard over the years from homeowners who chose to add options after the fact.

Finally, the location is also your choice, depending on the availability of homesites/lots in the community, for the home you choose. If you have a preference of an East, West, North or South exposure, be sure to keep in mind your lifestyle. This seems like common sense but is often missed and probably one of the most important things to consider when choosing your homesite/lot. Do you enjoy the sun in the morning peeking through your breakfast room, or gorgeous sunsets on your patio in the evening? Most people know this, but it is worth saying, the sun rises in the East and sets in the West, so choose wisely.

"A house is built with Boards & Beams;

a home is built with Love & Dreams."

- Author Unknown

THERESA FOWLER WEBB

CHAPTER 4

NEW-TO-YOU

FOUR ~ New-to-You

Brand New or *New-to-You*? This is an important question. The construction of a new home can take a year or longer. If you don't have the desire to purchase a newly constructed home, or the time to wait, and are ready to begin your new and exciting life *now*, *New-to-You* may be your answer.

A Well-Established Community

A well-established community can offer as many great features and benefits as a newly constructed community and may also offer a more *mature* sense of community.

A well-established community is just that, a community which has "settled in" and blossomed. There is no active construction, all homes are built and occupied, and the landscaping has matured and flourished throughout the community. The amenities are all in place and any activities or clubs are already under way. If offered, the monthly newsletter, with up-to-date information about clubs and activities, is available for your perusal, and everything will be accessible to you once you move into your new home.

Unlike a newly constructed home, there may be limited opportunity to customize your new home. All you do is move your furniture in, or possibly the home you purchased includes furniture, and voila, you can begin to enjoy your new home and life instantly!

Of course, you can make the decision to renovate the master bathroom or kitchen after you move into the home, but a venture of that sort will be *your* responsibility and not the Seller's, unless it was part of the Purchase Contract.

One of the greatest benefits of purchasing a previously owned home is price predictability. The home may already include such upgrades as freshly painted walls, new lighting fixtures, window treatments, and closet organizers, just to name a few. The home has been lived in and is already complete; thereby reducing the risk of any additional, unforeseen financial surprises.

Another consideration when purchasing a New-to-You home is exterior property changes. For example, if you are interested in adding a pool in the future, you will need to obtain a property survey from the seller or local municipality to determine if there is enough property to accommodate a future pool. To *add or change* any exterior elements which will affect the actual property, you will need to understand and comply with all the essential requirements set forth by the governing municipality.

In addition to obtaining all the necessary approvals through the municipality, you may also be required to obtain an approval from the Homeowners Association or Property Owners Association, should there be one in place.

A copy of the Declaration of Covenants, Restrictions and Easements or *any* applicable governing documents should be made available to you through the Seller. In these documents, you will find sections outlining the important rules and regulations, as well as information about *everything* governing the community. They will provide you with invaluable insight regarding what improvements you are able or unable to make *to and on* your property.

Think of it this way, the last thing you want to do is spend your hard-earned money on a new home and then find out you can't add a pool (or desired exterior feature) because it may violate some of the rules or portion of the governing documents.

Another item you will want to research is liens and assessments. Find out if there are any outstanding special assessments or special county/city tax liens for the community. If the previous owners failed to pay for the expenses for an improvement in the community, then *you will become* responsible when taking title to the home.

Additionally, inquire if there is an interview process and/or application which is required by the HOA/POA and any related fees. The Seller and your Realtor should provide you with all this information.

As you approach closing, the Property Management Company will provide the Title Company, Closing Agent or Attorney, any information regarding outstanding fees which the Seller would be subject to pay. It will also include any violations of the HOA/POA that the Seller may not have corrected, but is required to, prior to passing ownership to you. We will talk more about HOA's in Chapter 6.

When you have found the home and community of your choice, an inspection of the home is in order.

Some states, towns, and counties require different types of inspections on the home to satisfy their specific requirements, but more importantly, you should know *exactly* what you are buying. A good home inspection will include information about the structural integrity of the home, the condition of the mechanical HVAC, the electrical, the plumbing, the roof, and all major components. An inspection will be on your list of **MUST DO'S**.

Once the inspection is completed, you should review it carefully with your Realtor. The inspection will point out needed repairs or issues which should be corrected. You and your Realtor will discuss these items with the Seller and agree which party will be responsible for fixing them. Be sure to document these decisions in detail, should it modify or change the original terms of the Purchase Contract.

Also, ask the Seller or the Seller's Realtor if there is anything unusual about the *home* or the *property*, or any situation that may have occurred in the past which you should be aware of.

A good tidbit: If the home you are purchasing is under ten years old, there *may* be an existing dwelling warranty on the home. It may be prorated by the age of the home, but fortunately you would inherit it. This is a potential advantage of a *New-To-You* home.

If not, don't fret; there should be opportunities for you to purchase warranties during the process. Additionally, you may be the beneficiary of an *appliance service contract* which is still in effect. If the appliance is included with the home, the Seller will not benefit by keeping it. Inquire with the Seller, as they would be in possession of the original documentation for any warranties.

Before you know it, the time will come to close on the home and your dream will become a reality. The actual, physical closing *may* be handled by a third party, such as a Title Company or an Attorney. In today's digital world, you don't even have to be present to close on the home, but a walk-thru inspection of the home should absolutely be scheduled.

The walk-thru is your opportunity to confirm what you originally viewed when you purchased the home is still as you remember. Nothing has been destroyed in the home, nothing has suffered or died in the landscaping, and the home was maintained in the same physical condition and was not neglected in any way since the purchase.

You may have a reference guide to work from, as many of the homes listed in the Multiple Listing Service include photographs and even videos, which could work well for the comparison (should your memory fail you like mine does occasionally). I suggest you ask your realtor to share these photos with you. Soon you will be ready to move into your new home and begin enjoying your new life and lifestyle.

It would be quite impossible to list every fact, condition, detail or possible circumstance which may accompany the purchase of your new home. My goal is to reveal to you *some of the things* folks simply *don't consciously consider* when making a decision based on their emotions. I have touched on some of the areas *I f*eel are relevant and should be considered when making this important buying decision.

Interview with Ellen Burns – resident of an Active Adult Community.

Why did you move to an Active Adult Community?

I moved to be near my daughter and grandchildren. They live in a community very close to where we purchased.

When I first moved to Florida, I didn't know the area and for that matter, what type of community to look for. I did what most people do, I hired a Realtor who was a friend. Since I really didn't know what I was looking for, she directed me to an adult community. What she described to me sounded great, so we purchased a home in a small, intimate adult community. I was still working, and I really wasn't looking for any activities or lifestyle, so I didn't really mind when there was nothing to do... I just purchased a house.

However, when I did retire a few years later, I was more knowledgeable, and I wanted something more... I now understood what I was looking for in a community. I was fortunate my work involved managing property in Active Adult Communities... it seemed so very inviting to me.

I began my search, but this time I knew where I belonged. I knew what inspired me, and that was to live in the community where I had previously worked. When I began my search in the community, I instantly felt comfortable. The comfortability of the environment was the most compelling reason for making my decision to purchase a home in that community.

The Lifestyle offered was also very important and high on the list. I already knew the massive array of activities which could keep me very busy in my new retirement life. I also understood I could pick and choose my level of participation and involvement, which enhanced my comfort level.

We had a home buying budget in mind. Therefore, a good portion of the buying decision was driven by price. We were not both retired yet, but we planned to travel more once both of us retired, so we needed to keep that thought top-of-mind. We did not want a big mortgage. The new communities and newly constructed homes were slightly out of our price range and we wanted to reach our goal and travel more.

We began to look for a previously owned home. We did not want to renovate or tear the home apart, which would be just plain silly and counterproductive to our goal... as that costs money.

We needed something "middle of the road", comfortable and nice, in the community which felt right for us. In reality, we found what was most important to us, the perfect size home, in a cozy community, that offered the most value for us.

Now it's 5 years later and WE LOVE IT. We love to play cards and enjoy mahjong, twice per week, with a great group of people, and we expand that a bit and go out every couple of weeks to a movie or happy hour. I joined PAPS, a great Philanthropic organization, and I sit on the Board of Directors, which

I really didn't want to do... but they need my help, so I am there to help them. I am also on the Finance Committee because I can save the Association money... and I do.

Pearls of Wisdom shared by the interviewee

The most important thing I have learned but wish I would have known at the time I purchased, is my responsibilities as a homeowner concerning the maintenance of the grounds and how that compares to the responsibilities of the HOMEOWNERS ASSOCIATION. The community is maintained by the Homeowners Association, including lawn care, pest control, and maintenance of the amenities, but the details were not fully explained. For instance, the trees on the homeowner's property are maintained by the Association, however, should a tree die, it is the homeowners' responsibility to replace the tree. Also, the pest control is not on the interior of the home, only exterior, and it only includes the lawn and landscape, but not the perimeter of the home.

These are such little things, but they are the details, and the details can add up to dollars. A little more information would have been so much appreciated.

"I love my life." *If I can give one piece of advice, the most important thing that I can share is: if you are joining a community and you do not know anyone, JOIN EVERYTHING YOU CAN, EVERYTHING. If you don't JOIN EVERYTHING YOU CAN, you will be by yourself and that would be counterproductive when joining an Active Adult Community.*

My Take

She undoubtedly found everything she was searching for. She set her goals and created a plan to meet them.

She knew before diving in, that a newly constructed home was not within their budget, so she modified and adjusted her expectations about the home which would fit within their home buying budget. What I heard from her is - it is important to find a place where you will be comfortable.

Do the research before making your decision and know what will work for you and your home buying budget. Once you have a clearly defined budget, you will be able to make the best - informed decision which meets your budget and needs, and you may find that a previously owned home may very well be your answer too.

Be sure to understand the inner workings of the community and the HOA/POA. Be as informed as possible. Get involved with something you enjoy and love and have a great time with it. You and only You are the key to your new life... so make it count. It really doesn't get any better than this.

"The longer I live,

the more beautiful life becomes."

- Frank Lloyd Wright

CHAPTER 5

YOUR DOLLARS AND SENSE

FIVE ~ Your Dollars and Sense

Your search for the perfect home, in the perfect community, should be starting to take shape. You should now have a keen understanding as to *where* you would like to build your new life and *what* community will serve your interests and desires best.

Now it just comes down to the dollars. Remember the interviewee who had a certain home buying budget in mind, which benefited her future goal of wanting to travel more? She certainly got it right; *she planned with the end in mind*. If you work backwards like she did, then you will be more prepared and possibly avoid any financial surprises down the road.

First, decide on the amount of dollars you are willing to commit for the purchase of your new home. You may be saying to yourself, gee, that's easy... I have a good idea what I can afford which is great, BUT I want to review a few items which you might not have considered.

My goal is to limit financial surprises you may be faced with at the closing on your new home; in addition to touching on some of the reoccurring costs which you *may* incur while living in an Active Adult Community.

Having the good sense to ask these questions will make the most of your dollars.

Additional Costs

Each state and county have their own unique requirements, fees, and charges related to the closing of your home. These *Closing Costs* may be different if you are the Buyer or if you are the Seller, and if you are paying cash or obtaining a mortgage.

If you are obtaining a mortgage, more variables *may* come into play. Depending on the amount of the loan, and the percentage of the loan compared to the value of the home, the cost to you may vary. If you would like more details specific to the area you have chosen to build your new life, go to:

SoAliveAfter55.com/ClosingCostHelp

Some typical closing costs *may* include, *but are not limited to*, the following:

- County, Town or State taxes (prorated and determined by area)
- Prepaid Expenses – may include Homeowners Insurance and Daily Mortgage Interest charges.
- Government Recording fees
- Property Insurance
- Title Search and Title Insurance for Owner (and Lender for a mortgage)
- Attorney Fees and Settlement Fees
- Escrow fees for Homeowners Insurance and Taxes (prepaid in advance)
- Taxes and other Government Fees
- Appraisal Fee
- Credit Report (Mortgage)
- Flood Certification

- Origination Fee (Mortgage)
- Home Inspections
- Quarterly Prorated HOA/POA Fees (if there is an HOA/POA)
- Survey

While these costs are common, you'll need good sense to make the most of your dollars.

If you are contemplating obtaining a mortgage, be sure to work with a reputable mortgage loan officer or consultant who can fit you with a loan tailored to your financial needs. There *may* be additional costs to you not mentioned above, so please go to the website mentioned above which will provide you with a more detailed understanding of costs.

Now, let's look at the possible financial responsibilities of living in Active Adult Community. The information provided below is not for *every* community, nor does it include *every* cost you *may* incur. The intention here is to provide you with some fundamentals which will help you gain a greater knowledge and understanding of some costs which could come up down the road.

Monthly HOA/POA fees

These are the fees you will be responsible to pay either monthly or quarterly and are specific to the expenses of the Association.

Examples of some of these expenses *may* be, but are not limited to, the maintenance of the sod, irrigation, trees, bushes, and general landscaping in the common areas throughout the community.

Additional expenses which you might incur are the

general maintenance of the recreation facilities, the street lighting, the entry feature, and the gatehouse. Property management and operations costs may also be incurred and are paid for by the home owners. Each community is unique with different expenses, which *may* include various items which are not listed. It all depends on the amount of property and improvements that require maintenance, repair or future replacement.

It is highly recommended you request a copy of the *Operating Budget* of the community and take some time to review it carefully. All expenses should be delineated in the Operating Budget, either by actual cost or by estimated cost. Whichever it is, you will gain some insight as to the overall cost of the operating expenses for the community and your monthly or quarterly portion.

Another type of Association would be a Neighborhood Association and would be a voluntary membership and *may* or *may not* include fees.

Dining or Café Fees

If the community you choose offers a dining room or a cozy café within the boundaries of the community or in the clubhouse, there *may* be some fees associated with that luxury. Depending on the community, you *may* be required to pay an ongoing fee, as a guarantee of the dollars you will commit to spending on dining. Typically, with the communities I have managed, it was an annual fee.

Golf Fees

If you select a community which offers a golf course

(or two) within the boundaries of the community, keep in mind there *may* be yearly golf membership fees. Some communities offer unlimited golf with the membership, but again, it depends on the community.

An Equity membership or Initiation Member fee is another potential expense to you and is typically a one-time fee.

Tennis

Tennis is a common amenity which *may* be available to you at no additional cost. However, some communities have fees attached and the fees might also include a social membership of some sort.

Miscellaneous

The miscellaneous category of fees is all about *your* options. It *may* include classes that you may want to participate in or possibly club fees.

Fitness classes, aerobics classes, ceramics and 3D Art classes, cooking classes, Women's Club, Men's Club, fishing Club, and a Bridge Club are all examples of miscellaneous fees. These classes and/or clubs *may* be offered, among many others, and *may* be at an additional cost to you should you choose to participate.

Holiday parties, Las Vegas type shows, lectures, and off-site events *may* also be activities available in your community of choice and could come at a price.

It is important to note the fees of the HOA/POA of the community are not optional. Should you purchase a home in a community governed by an HOA/POA, you will automatically become a member of the association and thereby you agree to respect the rules along with the obligation of paying any HOA/POA required fees or special assessments.

Other governing bodies, such as Neighborhood Associations, are not mandatory and are voluntary, informal and may not require fees.

However, the reoccurring costs *are* optional. *You* have the option to participate in as much as or as little as you choose, depending on *your* interests. The beauty here is *you* make the decision for yourself; there is no obligation.

Don't forget... there *may* be many activities offered that are *NO CHARGE* to you. For example, some of those activities may include playing cards, every day if you want, swimming, working out in the fitness area, jogging, having lunch at the outdoor café, and the list can go on and on, again, depending on the community you choose.

As you can see, there are many questions you will want to ask. For simplicity's sake, I have developed a worksheet to assist you with your questions and serve as a tracking mechanism of the costs you think you may incur. You can print out this worksheet, check items off, and track your monthly and yearly obligations during and while asking the questions.

SoAliveAfter55.com/DollarsandSenseWorksheet

Download and print a copy of your "Dollar and Sense Worksheet," This will help you stay organized and keep you engaged with the questions you need to ask, all on one page.

Interview with J. R. Smith – resident of an Active Adult Community.

Why did you buy in an Active Adult Community?

We were getting ready to retire and wanted to enjoy our lives in a climate where we could enjoy the weather rather than living our lives planning around it, as we had done for so many years.

Our children were all grown and busy building their careers and lives as parents. We came to the realization that it was time to make a move... and advance to our next stage of life. We really didn't know where it would lead us.

We began by doing a bit of research in areas which offered "the sunshine climate," which prompted more questions for us and more research. We narrowed our search to a few states to consider for retirement.

Our decision was quite easy, as we also considered the proximity from our children and grandchildren, in addition to the affordability of the areas. Over the next few months, we sold our existing home. We were ready to take action and move forward.

It didn't take us long to understand what excited and motivated us. We wanted to be in a community that offered lots of activities, and to be among people in our age category. We heard so much about these types of communities and felt we would fit in well.

We contacted a Realtor in the area and shared our "dream home" concept with her, in addition to providing her with a buying budget range.

Our financial plan was to pay cash for our new home, use the proceeds from the sale of our previous home... and still have some dollars remaining for "life" itself.

After we viewed a couple of Active Adult Communities, we fell head over heels in love with one particular community. It had the perfect home, which was on the higher end of our buying budget, "of course."

Like most folks, we went home that night feeling exhilarated but at the same time, a bit discouraged when thinking about the price of the home and how we really shouldn't be considering spending the extra money.

We worked very hard all of our lives and planned along the way, for the best retirement life we could manage. But how can we manage to pay for this and still have some financial freedom?

That evening all we kept thinking about was how the community offered everything we wanted, and we just kept contemplating... how can we make this happen??

And then a lightbulb went off. We thought, what about financing a portion? We had a mortgage on our first home, so why not now??

We got up the next morning and made the life-changing phone call; we contacted a Mortgage Loan Consultant to pursue a mortgage. Oh boy, what a smorgasbord of loans and financing options, to the point where we got a little confused.

Don't get me wrong, we learned a great deal about the various types of Mortgage financing available, Conventional 30 Year Fixed Mortgage, a Reverse

Mortgage, Adjustable Mortgages, and FHA/VA Mortgages to name a few.

We were able to select a loan which fit our needs best. We were "back in the game" and raring to go again!

It has been six years now and we couldn't be happier. We are very active in the community and keep a monthly calendar on the refrigerator to keep track of each other... yes, we are that busy.

We both belong to clubs which meet monthly, we both play cards weekly and both do fitness training. It's so much fun and the health benefits of fitness training are great. We have both lost a few of those excess pounds we all seem to inherit as we get a bit older...what a great payoff and perk to simply having fun.

We have met so many new people, from all over the country and different walks of life and we truly enjoy them all.

We enjoy our grandchildren when they visit and take them to the clubhouse to show them off. **Everyone does!** *We all look forward to the Spring and Winter school breaks when the grandchildren visit. Grandchildren are a good part of most everyone's life in our community, so the community has special events for the children during the school breaks. How great is that???*

We engage in all sorts of activities and know in our hearts there is so much more joy to come. We love our community and feel we are now part of a very special group.

It's like nothing else we have ever experienced!

Pearls of Wisdom shared by the interviewee

The best advice I can share is "don't settle" if you really want something! On the flipside, don't be rigid and inflexible. I guess what I am really trying to say is to find balance in your plan. Regretting your decision because you settled is not fun at this point in your life.

However, you don't want to be house-poor either, as that may limit travelling or other activities you enjoy.

Our original plan didn't perform as intended, but we remained flexible and found a reasonable and balanced solution.

My Take

We obviously all want the best home for the best price. As of 2010 the Baby Boomers are retiring at a pace of 10,000 per day, so inventory is on the low end thereby creating a Seller's Market.

"Roughly 10,000 Baby Boomers will turn 65 today and about 10,000 more will cross that threshold every day for the next 19 years"

- Russell Heimlich

This may seem like a big number, but it's accurate, according to Pew Research and the Social Security Administration.

Finding what appeals to you and fits into your buying

budget may present some challenges in a Seller's Market. These folks were challenged but found their balance between lifestyle and a home. You don't have to choose between the two; buy a home within your means so you can still enjoy living your life.

If something is a "must have", look for alternative methods which will help you maintain the balance.

"Some people look for a beautiful place.

Others make a place beautiful."

Hazrat Inayat Khan

CHAPTER 6

RULES ARE NOT MADE TO BE BROKEN

THERESA FOWLER WEBB

SIX ~ Rules Are NOT Made to Be Broken

Living in a Homeowners Association (HOA) or Property Owners Association (POA)

Before we begin, I need to warn you, this chapter may contain terms and descriptions which could make you feel like you are reading an *operator's manual*. However, this information is important so pay attention. In my 20 years of experience operating and overseeing 9 Active Adult Communities, I cannot begin to tell you how many times violations occurred simply because the homeowner/member did not take the time to read the governing documents. As the adage goes, *"an ounce of prevention is worth a pound of cure,"* so take the time to be informed.

Be sure to read this when you are free of distractions because the content could save you some time, money, and frustration.

My goal is for you to gain a little familiarity with the subject of living in an HOA/POA; there is much more than meets the eye. The information below is *not* specific to *any area, HOA/POA or community* and simply provides *a basic and general* overview.

These are the topics *I feel* would be most beneficial for you as a new resident, treading in some unfamiliar territory.

Chances are you may purchase a home in a community which is governed by an HOA/POA or governing body. If that be the case, you will automatically become a member of the Association at the closing. Thereby, you agree to respect the rules and to assume the obligation of paying any HOA/POA required fees and/or special assessments.

I suspect you would welcome some insight about living in a community governed by an HOA or POA. Other governing bodies, such as Neighborhood Associations, are not mandatory memberships, they are voluntary and informal and not to be confused with an HOA/POA.

Many of the communities in the United States are governed by an HOA /POA or a governing body. Each community is unique and should have written and recorded documents. Those *may* include, but are not limited to, The Articles of Incorporation, The Declaration of Covenants and Restrictions, The Easements, The Bylaws, any Amendments, and Rules and Regulations of the community.

I know... you are scratching your head. This is foreign to many people, and this is a common reaction, so know that you are not alone.

I have provided a breakdown to introduce *some* basic fundamentals on community documents and living in a community governed by an HOA/POA.

Declaration of Covenants and Restrictions: This is the most comprehensive portion of the governing documents and provides general structure of the development. Additionally, it is the legal document which explains the guidelines of the community and is recorded in the public records.

Here you should find the legal description of the Property, including any preserve areas, along with the definitions of the community, and any community systems, such as, the cable system, the drainage system, the irrigation system, or the lake system.

It *may* also include definitions and descriptions of the recreational areas, the street lights, and the open spaces. Additionally, it *may* also share information regarding the rights of the property owner and the rights of the Association, the granting of easements, including utility, maintenance, drainage and buffers, to mention a few.

The Architectural Control Committee review and process *may* also be included in this section, along with the Association's responsibilities to operate and maintain the installed systems in the community.

Restrictions on leasing, owning animals and pets, parking, signs, and additions or alterations, including temporary structures, *may* also be covered in this section.

Prior to purchasing, you *should* obtain a copy of the governing documents of your community of choice and read through them thoroughly. The information is invaluable and may help you gain a keen understanding about what is permitted and/or restricted, in addition to what responsibilities you may have as a homeowner and Member of the HOA/POA.

Articles of Incorporation of the HOA/POA: These are the documents which created the Association and are filed with the Secretary of State where the development is located. They should provide definition, purpose and powers of the Homeowners Association, including Members and voting descriptions. It is typically brief and contains basic information.

Bylaws: The Bylaws describe how the HOA/POA operates and *usually* contains information regarding election and voting procedures of the members of the Board of Directors. They *may* also provide definitions and purpose of the "not for profit" organization and contain the powers granted to the Association.

Also included is information about Membership, Members' Meetings, and Voting and Proxies. It should contain specific insight to the powers and duties of the Board of Directors, outlining the rules with reference to the voting and counting of votes for the elections.

Critical information about definitions, power and duties of the Board, notifications to the members regarding all elections and any meetings of the Board of Directors should also be found in this area.

Please keep in mind, each community is *unique* and *may* or *may not* include all the areas of information in the governing documents and will vary depending on the community and *type* of Association.

Easements: What is an Easement? According to Merriam-Webster Definition, "an easement is an interest in land, owned by another, which entitles its holder to a specific limited use or enjoyment." An example would be a Utility Easement. A Utility easement is a certain portion of your property that grants permission to the Utility Companies, i.e. Cable, Gas, or Electric, to install their equipment and material, to provide you with service. You still own the property and enjoy it, but you are granting permission to the entity to install their equipment/material, in addition to granting the entity future access to perform any needed repairs on the equipment.

Rules and Regulations: These are the basic rules for the membership (remember each owner becomes a member when they close on their home) to adhere to, to live by and *to respect*. The general rules for the amenities should also be included. A good example is some general rules pertaining to the community Swimming Pools: no diving, no jumping, no food or drink on the pool deck, no nude bathing, etc.

This section will provide you with priceless information as to *what is* or *what is not* permitted in the community, and/or what items or actions on your part may require certain approvals.

One great example would be a future expansion on your home. You will need to know the following:

Would an addition or modification to your home be a consideration or permitted by the HOA?

Are there certain conditions which would need to be met regarding the construction and elevation of the addition?

Are there specific guidelines that would be imposed regarding roof type? (i.e. no flat roof permitted)

Are there any requirements regarding blueprints, construction plans, etc.? (i.e. architectural plans from a certified architect and a building permit issued by the appropriate authority)

Are there time frames of completion or deadlines associated with the improvement (30 days, 60 days, etc.)?

All this information is available. Just a few minutes of reading the governing documents will save you time, energy and *money.*

Another great example is pet restrictions. Do you have 3 pets? There could be a restriction which limits pets to only 2 per household. Having knowledge of the Rules and Regulations BEFORE you buy may come in handy and benefit you. It is a worthy read and will contribute to a greater understanding of the inner workings of the overall community.

The remainder of the governing documents usually consist of more facts and data and *may* include the HOA/POA Annual Operating Budget.

The Annual Operating Budget delineates, by line item, the yearly *projected* expenses (actual or estimated) of the Association. For example, items included, would be the insurance for the Association, the administrative expenses for the Association, the community website, the landscape maintenance of the overall community, the electric and the Recreational area expenses.

The Annual Operating Budget is the breakdown of the *projected* total annual operating expenses of the HOA/POA and calculates the quarterly and/or monthly dollar amounts to be charged to each homeowner/member.

Purchasing a home is most likely the largest investment you will make in your lifetime. If you are purchasing your new home in a community which is governed by an HOA/POA or any governing body, task yourself with reviewing the governing documents annually.

You should understand what you may be *buying and buying into.* Do some research and inquire if there are any outstanding special assessments, or if there are any upcoming major expenses/special assessments for the community you would be responsible to pay as a new owner. There is absolutely nothing to lose, and much to gain...you may be surprised as to how useful you may find the information.

Interview with Ken Solomon – resident of an Active Adult Community.

Why did you move to an Active Adult Community?

While we were still working, we vacationed in Florida every year. We would stay with our friends, who lived in a Country Club community of all ages.

When we were ready to retire, we purchased a home in the Country Club Community where we had visited yearly, where we felt comfortable.

We lived there for eight years when our friends decided to investigate a Brand New community, as they were contemplating a move. So, we went along for the ride.... or at least that was our original intention.

We had no plans of buying a home, but we did. We made the decision quickly, but not without some previous knowledge and discussions about making such a change.

An important factor was the location, as we had some family in the area and we wanted to stay close to them.

We were aware of all the benefits of living in an Active Adult Community. We like the idea of people in our age group with similar interests, and, of course, the amenities.

We were excited about buying a newly constructed home from a Builder with a great reputation. We were fortunate to have friends who purchased a home from this particular Developer/Builder. They shared how extremely impressed they were with the customer service and the care in which the Builder seized every opportunity to please their customers, which spoke volumes.

We are what you call snowbirds, or seasonals, which we prefer. We spend seven months of the year in our Florida home, which offers the most varied lifestyle.

Lifestyle, what is that exactly? My answer is "it is what you make it." One of the best ways to get recognized and involved in the community is to join a club, or volunteer for a community service... you will meet lots of people in addition to keeping busy, being involved, and positively impacting the community and its residents.

I personally decided to get involved with the HOA by joining the Architectural Committee. I felt my background and skill set were well suited to assist in this area.

Before I knew it, I was the Chairperson for the Committee and served in the position for about five years. As a Committee, we established procedural improvements and a consistent foundation of review and consistency of community, which is still in-tact today, and is easily recognized through a simple drive throughout the community.

I very much enjoyed working with the residents, searching for alternatives should their requested improvement not meet with the requirements set forth by the community guidelines and rules.

I felt I was helping to make a difference and having a substantial impact on people's enjoyment and the overall community. In addition to being involved, I had the opportunity to meet residents and made so many friends.

I thoroughly enjoyed every moment, and I continue to stay involved with many other projects, like clubhouse renovations, café, etc. SIMPLY LOVE IT!

Pearls of Wisdom shared by the interviewee

Active Adult is a real term which emphasizes the word ACTIVE, implying there is something for everyone. You never have to sit at home or be by yourself, because a friend is just a few steps away.

Sharing is the biggest hobby in an Active Adult Community and is one of the most wonderful features. It provides a lifestyle that includes what you want it to include.

It's unique to you! You have options... do you want to go to a baseball game with a group of neighbors or possibly out to the movies, join in a Poker or Canasta game?

Depending on community type, your choices may be as plentiful as you choose. You create the lifestyle that makes you happy. Living in an Active Adult community is a prescription for good health! The happiest people don't act their age. You can be 60 years old and feel and look 80, or you can be 80 years old and look and feel 60 and be the epitome of happiness.

We have gained so many new friends and with so many different clubs, you can share many values and interests. It's sort of a senior educational experience and adds much to your LIFETIME ADVENTURE.

I have learned in spite of their backgrounds, people all seem to wind up in the same place at this stage of life. All this... and to top it off, someone will cut your lawn and trim your trees.

My Take

The HOA/POA is comprised of *the people, for the people, and elected by the people.* In essence, these are your neighbors who have a vested interest in the community operating efficiently. Everyone has unique skills or services which may benefit the HOA.

As you can see from the interviewee, he got very involved and volunteered his time and energy for the greater good of the community. The community benefited immensely from his knowledge, experience and willingness to stay involved and make a difference.

If you are interested in volunteering your time or running for a seat on the Board of Directors, be sure to understand that this type of position can present challenges. Remain focused on the best interest of the community, maintain reasonable expectations, and you will be equipped to avoid unnecessary frustrations.

Keep in mind, you don't have to be on the Board of Directors to have an *impact* on your community, as there are committees established for particular interests.

Committees are extremely impactful and contribute to the overall success and functionality of the community. If you should find a committee that appeals to you, by all means, *get involved*.

The beauty here is as a member of the HOA/POA, participation is not required but rather recommended as it is *your* way to have a voice in how your community functions.

"I always wondered why somebody
doesn't do something about that.
Then I realized I was somebody."

Lily Tomlin

CHAPTER 7

THE PERFECT FIT

THERESA FOWLER WEBB

SEVEN ~ The Perfect Fit

We have reached a very exciting part of the book. Let's Talk about *Community and Lifestyle – the Ultimate Marriage*.

We have already talked about some of the options you might find, but this chapter will identify and highlight a more complete list of the options *may* be available to you when living in an Active Adult Community.

All communities *differ* regarding amenities and the overall Lifestyle choices. The information provided is simply a *reference* for you and is derived from an actual Active Adult Community.

There are so many different types of communities you can choose from, and many of those offer some type of lifestyle activities. It could be as simple as a swimming pool with a cabana bath as the amenities, or as extreme and extravagant as a Golf Community offering golf, dining and lots of activities. Then there are those offering everything in between.

One benefit of living in an Active Adult Community is there are usually No Country Club Fees, No Equity Fees, or No Initiation Fees, like those associated with traditional country clubs or golf clubs.

The HOA monthly/quarterly fee is your portion of the Annual Operating Budget which supports the overall operation of the community.

In the Active Adult Community, there is no golf course to support and the dining is usually very informal, similar to a café style. There are generally no Golf Membership Fees or expensive Dining Fees, although some communities *may* offer golf as a no-cost benefit or *may* include a cost in the monthly/quarterly fees. Should there be a dining fee in an Active Adult Community, it usually acts as a guarantee to the vendor and may be a small yearly amount (like $250/$300 per year).

Again, all communities offer different styles of living, different fees and memberships, and are usually based on the *type* and *number* of amenities offered.

So Alive After 55 is mainly focused on the Active Adult Lifestyle, which is maintenance-free living along with great amenities, events, and lots of activities and clubs to join.

I have referenced a lot of activities and clubs throughout the book, and it now time to share what some of those might be. The lists below are examples of the amenities, activities, and clubs offered at some of the Adult Communities that I have managed and operated.

Examples of Amenities

- Tennis Courts, with Tennis Pavilion
- Pickleball Courts
- Resort Style Swimming Pool with Pool Deck and Shade Cabanas
- Swimmer/Exercise Pool
- Resistance Walking Pool
- Clubhouse

- Grand Ballroom for entertainment and parties
- Café
- Fully Equipped Fitness Center
- Yoga and Aerobic Center
- Arts and Crafts Room with Kiln
- Demonstration and Catering Kitchen
- Jogging/Walking Paths
- Billiards Room
- Outdoor Whirlpool Spa
- Multiple Card Rooms
- ½ Basketball Court
- Grandchildren's Wading Pool
- Handball Courts
- Bocce Courts

Now just imagine some of the activities that could be generated from those amenities.

Examples of Activities

- Tennis Tournaments/Round Robins
- Tennis Clinics
- Cooking Classes
- Movie Nights
- Informative Lectures
- Holiday Parties/Events
- Barbeques
- Water Workouts
- Canasta/Bridge/Poker Card Games
- 3D Art Classes
- Ceramics Classes
- Personal Training
- Headliner Shows
- Trivia Night
- Wine & Cheese Parties

- Dancing
- Acrylic Painting
- Pilates Classes
- Aerobics and Zumba Classes

Examples of Clubs

- The Women's Club
- The Men's Club
- Dog Lover's Club
- Dining Club
- Ping Pong Club
- Musical Club
- The Bronx Club
- Various Philanthropic Clubs
- Photography Club
- Golf Club
- New England Club
- Wine Club
- Men's Softball Club
- Pinochle Card Players Club
- Pickleball Club
- Single's Club
- Fishing Club
- Men's Canasta Club
- Women's Canasta Club
- Ladies Golf Club
- Current Events Club
- The Pap Corps. (Champions for Research)
- Baby Boomers Club
- Cinema Club
- Duplicate Bridge Club
- Veterans Club

Please know the lists above *do not* include *all* the

activities, amenities, or all the clubs which may be available at any community. It is just a *representative collection* of activities.

By now you should have some useful insight as to the Lifestyle that may be offered in an Active Adult Community and could be awaiting you. Keep in mind, all communities are *unique* and differ in *style, size, homes,* and *amenities,* but the general *concept* is similar.

The list above consists of activities which were offered in the 9 communities I managed as VP for over 20 years. A list of these communities can be viewed at

SoAliveAfter55.com/ActiveAdultCommunities

During my twenty years working with the Active Adult buyer, I would often say, "*Anyone can build a house, but combining the perfect home with the ultimate in lifestyle is truly the key…. It's all about the Lifestyle."* I strongly believed in those words and believe in them even more so today.

I have personally observed positive developments in so many lives, such as the genuine pleasure so many have discovered, living in the Active Adult Communities.

Each person I interacted with was unique and yet also shared some commonalities with others. Many residents have shared their new life stories with me about how their quality of life became so enriched and celebrated, simply by "living" in an Active Adult Community.

I feel it is noteworthy to mention the remarkable

synergy and *cohesiveness* I was fortunate enough to observe, which seems to easily develop in these types of communities. It is truly wonderful.

*It's all about the Lifestyle...*which goes back to *you* and what *you* want and desire!!

Interview with Franni – resident in an Active Adult Community.

Why did you move to an Active Adult Community?

We had planned a trip with my sister to visit some communities in Florida, as she was looking to retire and relocate to Florida.

My sister instantly found the perfect community, and wouldn't you know it, I fell in love too.

My husband and I had absolutely no plans to move, nor had we any plans to retire yet. But we knew after being exposed to the Active Adult Community concept and the lifestyle offered, it was attractive and enticing to us.

The idea of an Active Adult Community was new to both of us, but we were intrigued. With so many things to do and activities to participate in we imagined ourselves living that type of life.

We were so captivated and excited, we decided to sample the lifestyle and purchased a vacation home in the community. We felt this action would serve in determining if we would enjoy Active Adult Living and help us ascertain if it was appealing and pleasing enough for us to consider as a permanent move.

Of course, it could not have worked out any better

than we had imagined. The community and lifestyle actually exceeded our expectations. We became permanent residents almost immediately.

My sister was a widow when she bought her home in the Active Adult Community and she has since found an unbelievable level of support among others in the community. She feels that she is not at all alone.

She has met other women who are also widowed, and all are of the same opinion, mainly because they all have each other and support each other. They get together and participate in many of the social events offered.

I personally feel such a sense of comfort knowing she has filled her life with close, dear friends and she enjoys and shares good times through the social activities offered.

She has found her own...and she treasures living in an Active Adult Community, with such a great level of support and friends who are like FAMILY!

Lifestyle was a key driver in our decision to buy a home in an Active Adult Community. We delighted in the idea of interacting with people our own age, with similar life experiences. We were very excited about joining clubs and participating in community events and social gatherings/parties. What's not to be enthusiastic about? What's not to LOVE?

Now that we have been here for over 10 years, our family and in-laws are beginning the search for their perfect community. It's obvious to us where they should be considering, and we have shared with them what we have learned. What could be better than living the active life with your friends, and now with family?

We enjoy our life to its fullest degree!

I do not know any people who wouldn't want to live in an Active Adult Community. People seem more open in this type of community, possibly because they aren't working, so they have more time to devote to establish and kindle relationships.

There is a fabulous feeling of togetherness. My thought is - people want to be friendly and get to know other people. It's what makes the world a better place.

Pearls of Wisdom shared by interviewee

When I first moved into the community, I met a woman at a social event, through another woman. I didn't have much time to get to know her that day, but I wanted to... she seemed so interesting. During our brief conversation, she mentioned to me where in the community she lived.

One day I decided to drive to her home and knock on her door. There was no anxiety, no nervousness, just excitement. We have been good friends ever since. Be friendly and shape relationships is my message.

You want to have people around. Remember, you are not alone. There is always someone to chat with or have lunch with. You will get to know pretty much everyone in your community because there is a place to hang out with everyone. Lifestyle is Everything!

Interview with Sandy Posner – resident in an Active Adult Community.

Why did you buy in an Active Adult Community?

We had 10 children between the two of us (second marriage) and 22 grandchildren. We were originally from the Northeast and moved to FL and lived close to the beach.

My husband loved the beach. The area really wasn't doing it for me. After a while, and after a few discussions, we decided to look around for a home in a different location.

One afternoon, we went to lunch with our cousins at a Country Club, which was in a family-oriented community, and the people at the table next to us were a young couple with baby triplets. We were distracted numerous times by the normal things babies do... cry, scream, cry and scream some more.

That was the moment, the moment that convinced us we wanted to live our lives among adults. Between the two of us, we had raised 10 children, and it was now our time.

We both agreed we wanted something different, more appropriate to our stage of life.

We had heard about Active Adult Communities and loved the concept. Enjoying our future days among like-minded adults was now a priority. We constantly saw newspaper advertisements boasting about Active Adult Living. So, we decided to check it out.

The rest is history. We purchased a Brand New home, to be constructed, in a Brand New Active Adult

Community.

We loved the overall-plan of the community and the concept of lifestyle that was defined and envisioned. Those two components were our motivators. We were exhilarated by the thought of becoming part of a community which was basically designed for Active Adults.

We purchased the largest home available, keeping our future family visits in mind. Good thing we did... as we have had a houseful of company, many times over the years. We had a great experience building the home of our dreams and it really is!

This part is funny, my husband never played tennis in his life, but before I knew it, he was learning to play. He became very good and enjoyed it immensely. Very quickly, he was playing six times per week. When my husband would come home from playing tennis, he would jump in the pool to cool down. He really enjoyed his new life.

I, on the other hand, am a very social person and wanted to meet new people and make new friends. It was important to me, as I feel very alive and charged around people, especially friends.

As I previously mentioned, we have a pool in our yard, but I decided to go to the community pool and make some new friends. It didn't take me long as I make friends very easily.

From then on, I got involved in everything I could. In fact, I made so many friends, and got so involved in so many aspects of the community, that my nickname became The Mayor.

Pearls of Wisdom shared by the interviewee

I lost my husband six years ago, and I am now without him. But I do not feel I am alone at all. I have made so many friends over the years and continue to keep busy, that it is difficult to feel any sense of loneliness.

Do I wish my husband was still here? Every single day. But I have now filled my life with wonderful friends who I consider family and keep busy with lots of activities.

The Lifestyle offered in my community plays a key role in my life. It keeps me going. It is such a wonderful feeling knowing there is something to do every day, anything can be on the agenda and I look forward to all of it.

I look forward to the activities, the events, and card games, and best of all I look forward to being with my friends. I make it a part of each day to participate to my capacity because I love the way it impacts my daily life and the way it makes me feel. I am always in a Happy Place!!

You have to become involved. It will keep your mind going. I am busy six days a week, either playing mahjongg, canasta, or making more friends at the pool. I attend all the shows and participate in everything... everything!

My Take

In our younger years, we tend to have priorities that are centered around building our life. Whether it's rising through the ranks in a career, enhancing one's craft or skill, or simply raising our children to become productive members of society, we are all building something called *"life"*.

When we reach the age of retirement, there seems to be a shift in priorities because, for the most part, our life is built and suddenly things begin to settle down a bit.

It is then that life tends to remind us of the things which matter the most but are often taken for granted.

Things like, family, friends, and sense of community seemed to be the common denominator with those I interviewed here, and my guess is it's the same for most people at this stage of life, *and that is a really good thing*!!

"*I don't wait for the calendar to figure out*

when I should live life."

- *Gene Simmons*

THERESA FOWLER WEBB

CHAPTER 8

YOU HAVE ARRIVED

THERESA FOWLER WEBB

EIGHT ~ You Have Arrived

It's time to pull it all together. Let's focus on making the journey as pleasurable and simplified as possible. This chapter is dedicated to doing just that, by condensing and summarizing the previous seven chapters into one easy-to-digest version.

I'd like to share with you my 20 years of Active Adult Community experiences and create a real-world application vs. opinion or conjecture.

Is This for You?

When we started this journey, I primarily focused on your *WHY* and your understanding of *WHAT*. *Why* do you want to live in an Active Adult Community and how would that impact your life, *and what* would Active Adult Community living offer you at this stage of your life?

At this point, you should have a much greater understanding of your *WHY* and *WHAT*, in addition to enjoying a sense of comfort. Are you ready to begin this exciting journey?

Perhaps you connected with or shared some of the very same feelings when you read the interviews and are now able to envision yourself sharing in similar experiences. Or perhaps you have an overall feeling of great eagerness and anticipation knowing what is available to you at this next stage of your life.

Whatever your *WHY* may be, *count on it* to act as your guide to direct and lead you to the community and home which is right for you.

In one of the Active Adult Communities I managed, I recall one individual who had some serious misgivings about the purchase of her new home.

She shared with me her doubts were based on her *fear* of leaving a neighborhood where she had many friends; she was now struggling with second thoughts about leaving them behind and moving forward. Although tempted to stay and somewhat conflicted, she did not turn back. Instead, she decided to see it through and took a chance.

To her surprise, she was in my office a month later absolutely elated and overjoyed about the life she was experiencing. She was tickled pink as she shared her delight with me. Overcome with excitement and emotion, she *had tears in her eyes*. I was so happy for her and her new-found life that I also had tears in my eyes.

To this day, we make it a point to stay in touch and do lunch occasionally. She always has a huge smile on her face and cannot stop sharing her adventures with me. I really enjoy hearing her experiences and continue to feel strongly that she made the correct choice for her life... and so does she.

Location, Location, Location

Location, Location, Location, offers valuable insight and *mindful* considerations when contemplating *where* you may desire to live your new life.

First and foremost, you must *make a commitment* to the specific area you wish to settle in. *Be true to yourself,* consider your priorities, preferences and the proximities to areas that interest you.

An experience with one couple comes to mind. My recollection is they specifically selected an area because it was near *two airports.* They were planning to travel frequently, back and forth to the Northeast to see their children, which was their *top priority*. Their family meant a great deal to them.

When we spoke, many of the conversations involved their children, such as one of their daughters was getting married and the excitement they were feeling, and many similar conversations.

They decided to select a location situated between the two airports, which still serves them well today. One of their children moved close to them but the other is still living in the Northeast.

As far as location goes, in their case, location was relative to airport convenience and *very important* based on their travel needs. They chose well.

It's your turn for some self-reflection, dig deep into your heart and recognize what your top priorities are. Your preferences will guide you when making location decisions; listen to the needs and desires of your heart.

As Jimmy Buffett said, "*Without geography, you're nowhere,*" and I concur.

Brand New

Brand New - A Brand New Home constructed by a Builder of your choice will offer you some opportunities and advantages. Depending on the Builder, you should be able to customize parts of your home to your liking.

I have found working with newly constructed homes in the Active Adult Communities that many were energized by the building process. They felt they were able to "shape" their home right down to the last detail, becoming an integral part of the process. Some owners would even go to the home when the slab was just poured and drop "good luck" coins into the slab or inscribe their initials in it.

Another couple I worked with had a large, beautiful home with everything imaginable, but they were not happy. Their community of choice offered no lifestyle and was comprised of predominantly seasonal residents. They wanted to enjoy their neighbors, but they were only there a few months of the year.

They decided to find a community which would offer them the lifestyle they felt they were missing and build a home that was just as beautiful and grand as the one they were currently living in. They showed up one day and requested a review of some plans.

They were obviously informed and wondered if it was possible to enlarge the home *prior* to purchasing. They were not going to commit to purchase without understanding the guidelines of the community.

They built a beautiful home, individualized to their taste and enlarged to their liking, but only after planning and submitting the various approvals required by the HOA for such an undertaking.

New-To-You

A previously owned home in a well-established, mature community has many advantages. Mature neighborhoods come with mostly previously owned homes, along with *established activities, clubs*, and *other amenities.* If you are looking for instant excitement and recreation, this may be your answer.

Another experience I encountered was with a couple who did not want to wait for a clubhouse to be built or the social aspect of the community to form. This is the case in most Brand New communities, unless you are purchasing after a majority of the community is already built.

The couple was ready to purchase on the spot. Their priority was to begin living the lifestyle and enjoying the activities *immediately*. THAT was their priority and they kept if front and center!

I remember them confiding in me and sharing how important it was for them to get *settled in*, make some friends, and get involved, so they could feel some of positive energy and start living their new life.

They indeed purchased a home in a well-established community where everything was complete. The Tennis Courts and Clubhouse were bustling, some clubs were already formed, a variety of classes were available, and the community offered a full calendar of events.

The couple found that a previously owned home in an

Active Adult Community was the way to achieve their number one objective.

Your Dollars and Sense

There is so much more than price to consider when purchasing a home. The closing costs and re-occurring costs are two *basic* expenses which you will encounter if you purchase in an Active Adult Community.

Closing costs come with just about every new home purchase but re-occurring costs *may* be tied specifically to community for HOA fees, activities, and events. Keep this in mind when planning your finances. You want to be able to enjoy your life and lifestyle.

Numerous times over the past 20 years, I heard about people who had previously lived in communities which included obligatory fees for golf or other types of memberships, but they had lost interest and were no longer participating in those activities. It may have served them well originally, but they found the on-going expense and fees were now unnecessary or even *burdensome*.

Active Adult Community living became very attractive and appealing to them, offering lower HOA fees and no membership type fees. They were able to positively impact their re-occurring expenses while safekeeping the social aspect of their life, all by choosing to live in an Active Adult Community and enjoy the lifestyle it provides.

Rules Are NOT Made to Be Broken

During my 20 plus years working with Active Adult

Communities, I found very few buyers take the time to read the documents that govern the community in which they purchase.

On the other hand, as President of the HOA of all 9 communities (until it turned over to the members at 90% closed) I made it a point to read through each set of documents from cover to cover.

I would go as far as indexing the documents for easy, quick reference. I am *not* suggesting you do this, but rather *strongly emphasizing* the *significance* and *value* of the information contained in the governing documents.

One good example of their value comes from a resident who decided to install a hedge along the entire rear and sides of his property, thereby creating a living fence.

It was quite a lot of hedge material, as you can imagine. He was unaware of any restrictions and did not submit any of the required documents to the HOA. Consequently, the hedge material did not fall within the guidelines of the Rules of the Association and had to be removed and replaced with approved hedge material.

The resident had to bear the cost of the original material, the *removal,* the *re-installment,* and the cost of the new material. Don't be one of the uninformed! Why even take a chance? These types of frustrating issues can easily be avoided by reading through the Rules of the Association.

It will serve you well and become a very valuable resource should you plan on making any improvements to your property... even if the improvement is as minor as adding a tree, which in many Homeowners Associations is not considered *minor* at all.

The Perfect Fit

As I often say, *"Anyone can build a house but combining the perfect home with the ultimate in lifestyle is truly the key... It's all about the Lifestyle."*

After more than 20 years observing and engaging with the Active Adult, what does Lifestyle mean to me?

The best definition I could formulate would be, "People living life to their fullest capacity while embracing the immeasurable benefits along with the vast opportunities of socializing and engaging in meaningful relationships which thereby creates belonging and opportunity for more human connection."

Human connection has so many levels. Developing close and interpersonal relationships can also be characterized as a form of bonding and can have a sincere heartfelt impact on one's life. Making friends and connections holds strong personal value, and in addition, may offer some great health benefits.

"Maintaining positive, warm and trusting friendships might be the key to a slower decline in memory and cognitive functioning, according to a new Northwestern Medicine study. You don't have to be the life of the party, but this study supports the theory that maintaining strong social networks seems to be linked to slower cognitive decline." said senior author Emily Rogalski, associate professor at Northwestern's

CNADC. (3)

And there you have it, and what a great benefit to Active Adult Community Living! In addition to enjoying activities, and sharing time with friends, comes great health benefits.

Wrapping it Up

My purpose in writing this book is to raise the level of awareness about what options are available to you at this stage of your life. My goal was to provide you with a better grasp of the concept and some basic instructions for Active Adult Community living. Additionally, I wanted to help you identify your priorities and preferences which will greatly influence your decision.

After gathering your thoughts, determining your *WHY and WHAT* is all you really need to do. There is no need for further speculation.

Find your balance... go deep into your heart and you may find that you are *ready* to go. Once you are ready, you must determine if you are *willing* to put in the time and effort for research and planning. You must be willing to depart from your current environment as many others have done and have shared in this book.

Last, but certainly not least, you will need to decide if are you *able.* Be sure to consider such things as selling your current home or having funds tied up, while determining if you are indeed *able.*

Is Active Adult Community living something that invigorates and moves you? By now, you should have at least started to answer the question. If you still have doubts, go back to Chapter 1 and find your *WHY* or speak with someone living the lifestyle.

If you ARE aware of your *WHY* and realize Active Adult Community living is for you, then seize the opportunity and take the first step.

Don't suffer from *analysis paralysis* because you want to have everything planned out in advance.

As with most new ventures in life, your plans will most likely evolve or change completely as you move through your journey... so just START!! The questionnaire in the next chapter is designed for just that, so be sure to use it as a guide.

As you may already know, Southeast Florida is a major retirement destination. The 9 Active Adult Communities I managed as VP, are located there. Those communities are listed at

SoAliveAfter55.com/Communities

If you would like to view any of the properties listed for sale on the community pages there, feel free to contact me.

I invite you to engage with me via social media, the places you can connect with me are listed on

SoAliveAfter55.com

> *"And in the end,*
>
> *it's not the years in your life that count,*
>
> *it's the life in your years."*
>
> *- Abraham Lincoln*

Questionnaire

Narrowing Your Search, Maximizing Your Time

This short questionnaire is designed for those who are ready to consider the Active Adult Community Lifestyle. It is designed to get you thinking about your options and help you start the planning process.

If you prefer to keep you book squeaky clean, you can find a similar questionnaire on our website, with the added benefit of submitting it for additional guidance. I look forward to being of service to you.

SoAliveAfter55.com/Questionnaire

First Name: _____

Last Name: _____

Are you interested in a warmer climate? Do you want to be close to areas of interest? Select your preferences below.

_____ Warm Climate

_____ Cold Climate

_____ City/Metropolitan Area

_____ Suburbs

_____ Close to Airports or Seaports

_____ Close to Shopping and Dining

_____ Close to Cultural Arts

_____ Close to Beach

What type of community do you prefer?

_____ Small, Intimate Active Adult Community

_____ Larger Active Adult Community

As we discussed, there are advantages to both the newly constructed home and the previously owned home. Select your preference.

_____ Newly Constructed Home

_____ Previously Owned Home

What location would you prefer inside a community?

_____ Lake View

_____ Garden View

_____ Close to Clubhouse or Tennis Area

_____ Private Yard

_____ Corner Lot

_____ Cul-de-sac Lot

What is your budget for your new home, keeping in mind the closing costs AND the reoccurring costs.

_____ $250,000 to $350,000

_____ $350,000 to $450,000

_____ $450,000 to $600,000

_____ $600,000 to $800,000

_____ $800,000 +

Are you planning to finance or pay cash for your new home?

_____ Cash

_____ Conventional Mortgage

_____ FHA/VA Mortgage

When would you like to move into your new home?

_____ 30 to 60 Days

_____ 60 to 90 Days

_____ 90 Days to 1 Year

_____ More Than 1 Year

Will this home be your primary residence or a secondary home?

_____ Primary Home

_____ Vacation Home

_____ Secondary Home

What type of home layout do you prefer?

_____ Single Family Detached – Single Story

_____ Single Family Detached – Two Story

_____ Single Family Detached – Multi Story

_____ Attached Villa

_____ Condominium

How many bedrooms would you like to have?

_____ 2 Bedrooms

_____ 3 Bedrooms

_____ 4 Bedrooms

_____ 5+ Bedrooms

How large would you like your new home to be?

_____ 1500 to 2000 square feet

_____ 2000 to 3000 square feet

_____ 3000 to 4500 square feet

_____ 4500 + square feet

What size garage do you need?

_____ 2 Car Garage

_____ 3 Car Garage

_____ 4 + Car Garage

Now for the fun part, what Lifestyle activities are you interested in?

_____ Activities (parties, dances, barbeques, fitness)

_____ Clubs (poker club, current events club)

_____ Shows (comedy, musical, or variety shows)

_____ Golf (in a community, one or more golf courses)

_____ Golf (outside the community but close)

_____ Tennis (tournaments, clinics, round robins)

_____ Security (front gate, in-home, on-site)

_____ Maintenance Free (exterior of the home)

_____ Pools (lap or swimming, indoor, outdoor)

_____ Card Games (poker, pinochle, canasta, bridge)

_____ Café or Dining (casual or formal)

_____ Social Gatherings (lectures, seminars)

_____ Outside Activities (hosted by the community)

THERESA FOWLER WEBB

Bonus Interviews

Interview with Sara Lisinsky – resident of an Active Adult Community

Why did you move to an Active Adult Community?

At first, we were thinking about living by the ocean and completely renovating an older home. As much as that sounded to us like something we would like, we quickly realized it would be a huge undertaking. We also had some concerns about being isolated and not having a sense of community. There are times that isolation, in any community, will most likely exist, however, we wanted to limit it as much as possible.

We were done with the cold, nasty winters, our kids moved away, and here we were, but now what?? I think many people pose the very same question... I believe it's a wonderment everyone seems to have at a certain stage of their life.

Another inspiration for us was we had family who lived in the area for over 35 years. I also lived in the area many years ago and had a little familiarity. We watched it grow over the years.

Now it was time to make the final decision... and we found the final decision was obvious to us after seeing our dream home on display in a model home center.

The opportunity to be able to build the home we really loved, with an array of choices and optional features to customize to our individuality, was extremely appealing to us. It was like music to our ears.

We also felt we could find the sense of community we were searching for, as this particular community was an Active Adult Community with amenities, activities, and lifestyle, all which were available to us.

We went through the building process, and it was a great experience. We customized our home as much as possible. It truly reflects us...We moved into our gorgeous new home and instantly began to get involved with the community activities. We found some things were very different than what we were accustomed to. Years ago, my grandmother lived in a similar community and she shared some great advice which helped us. "You need to know what is **comfortable** *for you and if you don't, you need to find your* **comfort zone***. Always stay true to yourself...you are who you are! And be okay with the results should people shy away."*

Everyone should have a great time, no exceptions!!!

Pearls of Wisdom shared by the interviewee

Be gracious and welcome the newcomers to the community. Invite them to share a table with you at an event... introduce them to friends and get to know them, their background, and their interests.

Find a few friends. In general, you may not agree with everything in the community, how it is planned or operated, but go with it... it all works. Go to meetings, stay informed, be open to different ideas, and be a good listener. People, at times, may be concerned with the good of a few, but remember, it needs to be for the good of many.

Find your niche. It will be a work in progress... and that is part of the beauty of it all. You need to figure out what you want to do, and you will; have fun with it.

We are very happy. We love where we live, and we love our home. If you're not happy in a community that offers a "sense of community", in addition to a multitude of amenities coupled with an active, fun-filled lifestyle, then maybe you're just not happy.

My Take

The interviewee mentions finding your comfort zone and understanding what is comfortable for you, and I certainly concur. With change comes challenges, and if you understand your comfort zone, you can overcome those challenges with some ease.

A bit of excitement may often accompany change which may create the balance we all yearn for when we are faced with major change. "A work in progress" is a great way to describe the transition to the retirement stage, or simply to describe life in general.

One of my favorite stand-up videos is "When the doorbell rings today vs. 20 years ago" by Sebastian Maniscalco. Google it... he jokes about the unexpected visitor at your door and compares how different we react today vs. the reactions of 20 years ago.

Unfortunately, technology has influenced our lives in many ways... not just when we communicate, but very much **how**.

Back in the day of no cell phones and no internet, folks would just stop by for coffee and some of the Entenmann's cake mom saved just in case company dropped by; it was natural to welcome those visitors...with open arms. I remember this occurring frequently in my younger years. For most of us this is not the case today, but for me, being of the Italian tradition, it is quite abundant in my life.

In my opinion, Active Adult Community living is a means to bring that back... and so much more.

"The length of one's days matters less than the love of one's family and friends."

- Gerald Ford

Interview with Roberto – resident of an Active Adult Community

Why did you move to an Active Adult Community?

The main reason was basically retirement. There were other reasons which were also important including the area, the climate and the community.

I was very attracted to the 55+ Active Adult Community because I felt like there would be common ground. I was thinking I could make new friends, enjoy playing a game of cards, or go to some Vegas type shows.

I feel it's very important to find your kind of people... meaning, people with the same interests, in the same age category and even some of the same anxieties. Making friends can totally be an anxiety. Some people are afraid, but that seems to disappear as you enter the world of living in a 55+ Active Adult Community.

I couldn't imagine living in a community that is not an Active Adult Community. I couldn't imagine having neighbors who are just starting out their lives, working all week, and managing their households on weekends. Kids playing in the street... no, I couldn't imagine that at my stage of life.

It can be quite a challenge moving 1500 miles away... I didn't know the area well, so I did some homework. I wanted to understand the culture of the community I was moving to. I would contemplate over and over again, am I making the right decision on the home, the community and the area I chose? The homework served me well, and relieved most of the anxieties I was feeling... and then all I needed to do was to make the effort and go out and try it for myself. These types of communities foster involvement, mainly due to all the activities, the clubs, the parties, and the events you can join and participate in. The important message here is to plan and think ahead!!

There is nothing I would change... mainly due to the development of new friendships. When you are in your 50's and are looking to make a change, I cannot see anything other than moving to an Active Adult Community.

It is human nature to feel a little bit of fear especially when leaving your children and grandchildren... and we certainly did... but we worked it out in our mind that the grandchildren were in their teens and we would only see them for an hour or so a week. We didn't want to feel like we were leaving them... so we chose not to feel that way.

I have found that many people have never lived in an HOA or POA. It is something very foreign to them. I had a little knowledge and understood the general concept, which certainly helped me immensely. I would strongly suggest being sure you understand and maybe even get involved in the HOA. The act of getting involved will provide you with invaluable knowledge and you will be contributing to the community.

Pearls of Wisdom shared by the interviewee

There are many opportunities to make friends in an Active Adult Community. You don't have to be friends with everyone. Weed out those who have different interests or values.

Believe me, it makes a HUGE difference living in an Active Adult Community. The opportunities are vast. You can go fishing one day and be listening to a speaker providing insight on the conservation of water the next day. You choose what you want to do, when you want to do it, or not. But don't make excuses for not getting involved. So, go to the clubhouse, go to the restaurant and just say, "Hi," to someone.

Speak to people in the community prior to making your decision. Speak to those who have lived in the community for years and those who just recently became residents. Ask them the same questions...and understand their answers, and especially the differences in those answers, should there be any. Apply those that are relevant to you and your passions, to help guide your way.

You can't eat the soup without a spoon. This is it! You only get one shot... so enjoy it!

My Take

As the interviewee states above, doing your

homework up front is important. Follow his advice and take the steps he took. I would also encourage you to create a list of 'MUST HAVES' vs. 'NICE TO HAVES' to help assist you in your decision. One word of caution, in the essence of Jim Rohn's quote below, don't suffer from analysis paralysis seeking perfection. I can't tell you how many times during my 20-year career working with the Active Adult I witnessed people walking away from a home and lifestyle which was right for them simply because it wasn't quote "Perfect." The goal is to "check off" as many, if not all your "MUST HAVES" while gaining as many "NICE TO HAVES" as possible in the process.

"The time to act is when an idea strikes. Instead of waiting for perfect circumstances, or a day that may never come, create your own momentum."

- Jim Rohn

Interview with Ronnie and Sandy Kaplan – residents of an Active Adult Community

Why did you move to an Active Adult Community?

We moved here, to a warmer climate, due to health reasons. We went on vacation in Florida, and at the time, were selling our business. My business sold while we were on vacation, which prompted us to think about the possibility of renting a home or condominium in Florida part-time. For the remainder of 4 or 5 months of the year, we could enjoy our boat, which we were able to live aboard. Our journey began at the ocean, looking for a condominium. We fell in love with the idea of living near the beach. We found the perfect condominium and we were strongly thinking about putting down a deposit to rent.

We went to breakfast on our way to meet our Realtor one morning. As we entered the restaurant, I picked up a free magazine by the cashier, and saw an advertisement for an Active Adult Community which really caught my interest. The community was somewhat new, from what I could tell from the ad, and the ad boasted that, as a buyer, you would be able to select your location and be able to build your house of choice. We finished breakfast, delayed our appointment with the Realtor and off we went. Our mission was to visit the community and understand what this "active" life was all about.

Even though we didn't think we were ready to leave our "history" or our friends and family, the overwhelming feeling of this type of life overcame our concerns and was now in control. Long story short, we got so caught up in the emotion and the idea of the active life after understanding more about it, with so many activities and opportunities, we didn't think twice about it... we went ahead and purchased the home. We were so darn excited... beyond words... but once we got back home up North, to the real world, we asked ourselves, what did we do? We reacted and decided to cancel our purchase.

It was depressing... Ronnie really fell in love with the idea of activities and clubs at his fingertips and was not happy we were not going to take the leap. After a few days or so, the thought of "why" came to me...

why were we originally undertaking this adventure? Why were we so excited to a level that we committed and purchased the home? By asking myself these questions, it became clear.

Health was the priority reason. However, life and enjoyment of life was now a major factor in the decision. The community we had fallen in love with, was obviously the answer for us. My husband is my best friend, and his happiness means the world to me. So, the next day, we called the Sales Consultant and told her we made a mistake and were committed to the purchase of our new home along with our new life. And here we are...

What appealed to us... and why. The Lifestyle was extremely appealing. The lifestyle of meeting new people and making new friends was exciting to us. We left our history, our home where our kids grew up, our friends who we would meet up with at the park with their kids, and our business associates we shared our business life with. Friends can become your family. When you go to a new community, everyone wants to get together. Everyone is looking to be friends. We weren't looking for just a house. We wanted to have something to do.

Pearls of Wisdom shared by the interviewee

Wherever you go, there will be different groups who will share your interest, and then there will be groups who will not share your interest.

Communities grow. You make your life. We believe in giving back. Many people work hard and volunteer their time in these types of communities. Becoming part of a group of people working for a cause forges strong relationships.

What were our FEARS? We had no fears. Life is an adventure and this move was yet another adventure in our lives. How does anyone know in life what we are going to experience? Why not experience as much as you can?

*I have learned to appreciate people – to be open. We are not too old to learn something new, so we are never too old to **meet** someone new. Even though we left our history behind, we have made many great memories here.*

My Take

I think we all second guess ourselves at one time or another. Your intuition is based on years of experience, and often, experience is speaking to you. When we listen to our intuition, we do well. Fear or doubt, and second guessing ourselves at times, clouds our vision and how we see our lives. If you want clarification, go back to your *WHY* and start there.

Even though the interviewees experienced some self-doubt, they soon realized their *WHY* – what originally excited them and *WHY* they reacted. In the end, they chose to follow their heart, follow their *WHY*, and go for it.

"The best and most beautiful things in the world cannot be seen or even touched - They must be felt with the heart."

Helen Keller

THERESA FOWLER WEBB

About the Author

Theresa Fowler Webb was born in New York City and lived in the Bronx until she was twelve years old. She enjoys fond memories of her childhood days. She has three sisters, and remembers her dad working two jobs, and her mom working nights to put food on the table and stay afloat with four children. This might sound rough, but the situation strongly bonded the family and created the inner strengths that she and her sisters possess.

Today, Theresa owns her own company which is designed to assist the Active Adult prospect in evaluating, navigating, and determining whether the Active Adult Lifestyle is right for them. Prior to owning her company, Theresa worked for GL Homes for over 28 years, one of the most well-respected and largest privately held Builders in the nation.

For years, Theresa has talked about writing a book about her unique and exciting experiences. She has spent over twenty years working with retired (or soon to be retired) adults who were seeking their new home in their choice community. She managed and oversaw operations as Vice President for over *$3 billion* in sales and closings for nine Active Adult Communities encompassing over 6500 homes and has touched the lives of over *13,000* residents.

It all began in 1996, when Theresa earned the opportunity to conduct Operations as the Vice

President in an Active Adult Community. She immediately realized she had much to learn and was eager and ready for the challenge. Over the next 20-year period, Theresa was involved with many aspects of the planning, executing and overall supervision of the nine communities in addition to the daily Sales, Closings and Operational aspects. Theresa also assisted and was instrumental in developing various aspects of the "Lifestyle" offered at these communities.

Additionally, as President of the Homeowners Associations, she was intimate with the inner-workings of the communities and created educational seminars and workshops for the residents, thereby offering them an opportunity to better understand the various facets of an HOA and all it encompasses. The residents were always eager to attend her Community and HOA meetings, as she is a proficient speaker, but ever more so, an accomplished listener.

During the 20+ years, she acquired a wealth of knowledge about all that mattered to the Active Adult; mattered to their home and lifestyle and most of all, mattered in their life. Theresa has helped many customers navigate the transitioning process (from their old home and neighborhoods to their new home and new environment) which became very fulfilling for her and very much appreciated by them. She is known for her honesty and has demonstrated her trustworthiness and strong sense of *personal engagement* while consistently presenting fair and equitable solutions for all involved. Theresa remains in touch with many of her previous customers who she now considers friends.

Throughout the book, Theresa empowers her readers to make an informed decision about their next chapter of life – retirement. She offers insightful guidance and direction and has mapped out a simple route to conduct the search for your new life. Her *personal touch* along with her uncompromising passion confirms and reinforces her belief in *human connection* and she is exhilarated to share with you her vast knowledge in the world of "Active Adult Community Living."

Over the years, Theresa has witnessed a wide range of emotions which came from those considering this type of lifestyle change. Many Active Adults have spent their entire lives taking care of loved ones and that's a good thing; however, when it came time for them to take care of themselves, a sense of "guilt" was often accompanied with that desire. As a passionate mother, grandmother, daughter, sister and wife, from a large, traditional Italian family, Theresa intimately understands the importance of balancing the needs of the Active Adult with the needs of their loved ones. Let her be your guide in this next beautiful chapter of your life.

"I alone cannot change the world, but I can cast a stone across the water to create many ripples."
Mother Teresa

Bibliography

In the Preface

1. http://youngtownaz.org/index.aspx?NID=974

Uniquely Youngstown, AZ - Historical Museum

April 12, 2016

2. https://dewf.net/DEWForg/MrWebb/MrWebb.html

From Wikipedia

Del E. Webb Foundation (site)

Updated 2017-07-19

Article name: "Mr. Webb"

Del Webb's quote: When I see what we've built, it's the most satisfying thing that's ever happened to me."

In Chapter 5 -Your Dollars and Sense

3. http://www.pewresearch.org/fact-tank/2010/12/29/baby-boomers-retire/

Article: Baby Boomers Retire - Pew Research Center

"Roughly 10,000 Baby Boomers will turn 65 today and about 10,000 more will cross that threshold every day for the next 19 years"

December 29, 2010. Pew Research Center

By: Russell Heimlich

In Chapter 8 – You Have Arrived

Article about Health Benefits and Socializing – Northwestern University – Close friends linked to a sharper memory 'Maintaining strong social networks seems to be linked to slower cognitive decline'

4. https://news.northwestern.edu/stories/2017/november/close-friends-superager-memory/

November 01, 2017

By Kristin Samuelson

Northwestern Now

Made in the USA
Middletown, DE
12 August 2019